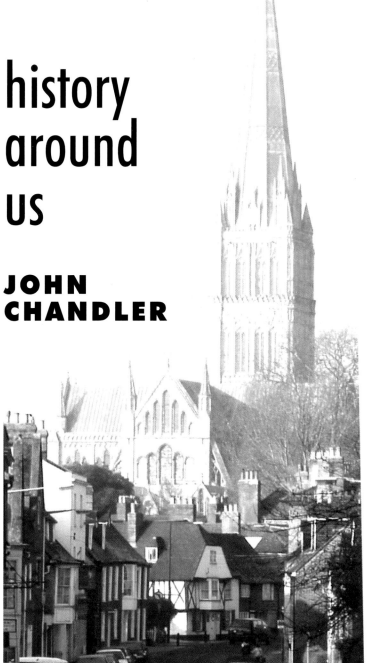

SALISBURY

history
around
us

**JOHN
CHANDLER**

First published in 1992, as *Salisbury: history and guide*, by Alan Sutton Publishing. This revised edition published in the United Kingdom in 2004 by The Hobnob Press, PO Box 1838, East Knoyle, Salisbury SP3 6FA

British Library Cataloguing in Publication Data
A catalogue record for this book is available from the British Library.

ISBN 0-946418-24-1

Typeset in ITC Officina Serif and Futura
Typesetting, photography and origination by John Chandler
Printed in Great Britain by Salisbury Printing Company Ltd, Salisbury

CONTENTS

INTRODUCTION

I OWE THE CONCEPT of this book to my friend David Buxton, then commissioning editor of Alan Sutton Publishing, who asked me to write a short history and guidebook to Salisbury as the prototype for a planned series of town histories. That was in 1992, and the resulting *Salisbury: history and guide*, has been out of print for many years. But interest in and affection for one of England's most attractive and historic cities remain as strong as ever, and at present there is no other short paperback history available to satisfy the curiosity of visitors and local people. I have therefore thoroughly revised my earlier text, reformatted the book's design with a new title, and included many more and different illustrations.

No city stands still, and nor does its history. Since 1992 there have been major new studies published of Salisbury Cathedral and Close; important archaeological investigations in the city, around Old Sarum and elsewhere; a further volume (three of a projected four) of Salisbury Museum's medieval catalogue; an edition of the earliest city ledger; two perceptive general histories; and (to date) three issues of a new annual historical journal, *Sarum Chronicle*, devoted to Salisbury and its surroundings. Local history is nothing if not dynamic.

The arrangement of this book is straightforward. Seven chapters describe Salisbury's evolution, from prehistoric hillfort, through regional capital of medieval southern England to tourist Mecca and shopping centre. A further pair of chapters offer guided walks to the Close and cathedral, and to the city centre.

John Chandler, East Knoyle, June 2004

DELVING DEEPER

IF YOU ARE A VISITOR to Salisbury you should call in at the city's award-winning Tourist Information Centre in Fish Row (behind the Guildhall) for details of access to buildings, museums and sites of historic interest in the neighbourhood. These include the following: Salisbury Cathedral; St Thomas's Church; Salisbury and South Wiltshire Museum, The King's House, The Close; Redcoats in the Wardrobe (military museum), The Close; Malmesbury House, Medieval Hall (Deanery) and Mompesson House, all in The Close; Old Sarum Castle; Stonehenge (10 miles north); Wilton House (3 miles west). A number of medieval and historic houses in the city now function as shops, inns and restaurants, and one is a cinema foyer. Under certain circumstances, therefore, such buildings are also accessible to the public.

Anyone wishing to explore Salisbury's history further should visit the Hugh Shortt Gallery in Salisbury and South Wiltshire Museum, and the Salisbury Local Studies Library on the first floor of Salisbury Library, in the Market Place. The library possesses a comprehensive collection of books and other material on Salisbury and Wiltshire, for reference use. Most archival sources for the city's history, including city council, parish and diocesan records, are held in the Wiltshire and Swindon Record Office, Trowbridge (but moving to Chippenham 2007/8). Other local repositories possessing archives relevant to Salisbury include Salisbury Cathedral Library and the Hampshire Record Office, Winchester.

In addition to my own larger work on Salisbury (*Endless Street: a history of Salisbury and its people,* Hobnob Press, 1983, reprinted 2001), there are two excellent recent histories of the city:

Ruth Newman and Jane Howells, *Salisbury past*, Phillimore, 2001

Bruce Purvis, *Salisbury, the changing city*, Breedon Books, 2003

The benchmarks for academic study of Salisbury's history are the following:

Royal Commission on Historical Monuments, *Ancient and historical monuments in the city of Salisbury*, vol.1 [the city], 1980; *Salisbury: the houses of the Close*, 1993; *Salisbury Cathedral: perspectives on the architectural history* (by Thomas Cocke and Peter Kidson), 1993; *Sumptuous and richly adorn'd: the decoration of Salisbury Cathedral* (by Sarah Brown), 1999 (all published by The Stationery Office, formerly HMSO).

Victoria History of the Counties of England: Wiltshire, vol. 3 [ecclesiastical history, including the cathedral and diocese], 1956; vol. 4 [economic and social history], 1959; vol.6 [includes histories of Wilton, Old Sarum, Salisbury and Fisherton Anger], 1962.

Older histories of Salisbury and important works on specific subjects include the following:

Tim Ayres, *Salisbury Cathedral: the west front*, Phillimore, 2000

R Benson and Henry Hatcher, *Old and New Sarum, or Salisbury*, 1843

Alison Borthwick and John Chandler, *Our chequered past: the archaeology of Salisbury*, Wilts CC, 1984

Charles Haskins, *The ancient trade guilds and companies of Salisbury*, 1912

Laurence Keen and Thomas Cocke (editors), *Medieval art and architecture at Salisbury Cathedral*, BAA Conference Transactions 17, 1996

M D Lobel (editor), *Historic towns*, vol.1 [includes Salisbury, by Kenneth Rogers], 1969

Nikolaus Pevsner (revised by Bridget Cherry), *Wiltshire*, Penguin 1975 (The Buildings of England)

Dora Robertson, *Sarum Close*, 1938

Peter and Eleanor Saunders (editors), *Salisbury Museum medieval catalogue*, parts 1-3, 1990-2001 (part 2 by Brian Spencer, part 4 forthcoming)

Hugh Shortt (editor), *City of Salisbury*, Phoenix House, 1957

Hugh Shortt (editor), *Salisbury: a new approach to the city and its neighbourhood*, Batsford, 1972

Many of these works include bibliographies which will lead the researcher to more specialist books and articles. In addition to the works listed above, there is much of use in the following series and serials: *Hatcher Review*, 1976-2001; *Sarum Chronicle*, 2001 onwards; *Wiltshire Archaeological and Natural History Magazine*, 1854 onwards; Wiltshire Record Society, 1939 onwards (especially vols 21, 30, 50, 54); and the publications of the Salisbury and South Wiltshire Museum, and the South Wiltshire Industrial Archaeology Society.

DR JOHN CHANDLER has been involved in the history of Wiltshire for nearly thirty years, and has written a major social history of Salisbury, *Endless Street*, which was published in 1983, as well as more than twenty books about aspects of local and regional history. He is general editor of the Wiltshire Record Society and co-editor of the *Wiltshire Archaeological and Natural History Magazine*. He runs Hobnob Press from his home in south Wiltshire, and is working on a history of the whole county, of which two volumes (covering Kennet District) have been published so far.

1

BEFORE SALISBURY

ON A SPRING DAY in the thirteenth century, at a pre-arranged place in a Wiltshire meadow, a group of distinguished clerics and noblemen gathered to lay the foundation stones of a new cathedral. By so doing they triggered a chain of events which resulted not only in one of the most sublime achievements of medieval architecture, but also in a city of outstanding interest and charm. The consequences of that birthday, 28 April 1220, are the subject of this book, and we shall watch the child grow and develop to maturity. But first we must look at its ancestry, and describe the world into which it was born.

The name given to the new city, Salisbury or New Salisbury, already belonged to the riverside estate on which it was established, and which extended several miles northwards up the valley of the River Avon. This estate was named in turn after its most prominent natural feature, a domed chalk hill jutting out towards the river from the high ground which separates the Avon valley from its neighbour, the Bourne. Although nobody is sure what it means, the first part of the name may be traced back through time (*Salis–, Saris–, Searo–, Soruio–*) to the Roman

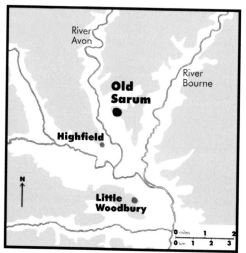

The Salisbury area in late prehistory, showing places mentioned in the text

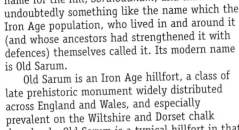

Old Sarum from the east, seen in a nineteenth-century engraving

name for the hill, *Soruiodunum*; and that was undoubtedly something like the name which the Iron Age population, who lived in and around it (and whose ancestors had strengthened it with defences) themselves called it. Its modern name is Old Sarum.

Old Sarum is an Iron Age hillfort, a class of late prehistoric monument widely distributed across England and Wales, and especially prevalent on the Wiltshire and Dorset chalk downlands. Old Sarum is a typical hillfort in that it has concentric rings of defences (two banks and a ditch) around a prominent hilltop, and like many others it was constructed in more than one phase. It was probably begun several centuries before the Roman conquest, and continued in use (of some kind) after they had arrived. Standing on the massive ramparts today it is possible to appreciate the tremendous community effort (whether coerced or voluntary) that must have been needed to make the hillfort, and also how much reassurance it could have provided for the farming communities who lived within sight of it along the valley or on the hillsides. Commanding as it did whatever river-crossings were in use in the valley it had obvious strategic importance, in addition to its role as a refuge for the local population. In happier times it probably served as a focal point for a territory, a shared centre of local government and justice, and perhaps a rudimentary market place or fairground.

Unlike the towering hillfort there is nothing now to see on the ground of the Iron Age farmsteads which it may have policed and protected. But plenty of archaeological and air photographic evidence has been found for their existence on the surrounding hillsides. One site, known as Little Woodbury (close to the modern District Hospital), was carefully excavated in 1938-9, and is regarded as the classic example of a small Iron Age settlement within an enclosure. Another, at Highfield (off the present Devizes Road), continued in use through much of the Roman period. Such farms were scattered across the high ground north of Old Sarum, too, and may also have existed in the valley. But here

Old Sarum's impressive earthworks

later farming activity, alluvial deposits, and the spreading city itself have tended to obscure them.

Any changes to farming and ordinary life which occurred in this settled valley after the Romans arrived seem to have been gradual and gentle. But the newcomers were responsible for two innovations which have left their mark on the modern landscape. Old Sarum was a sighting point used by the road surveyors of the Roman

The Roman road from Winchester survives as a minor lane approaching Old Sarum's eastern entrance

army soon after the conquest for the alignment of at least five roads. From the hillfort's eastern entrance we may still see three of them (now an A road, a B road, and a C road) heading towards us, and a fourth has given us the name Stratford ('the ford of the paved road'), which belongs to the village beneath the western rampart.

Stratford (or to give it its full name, Stratford-sub-Castle) is important in another respect too, because it was next to the site of the modern village that a small Roman town developed along a road which led down from the hillfort to the river. Many Roman towns were built close to important Iron Age centres (Dorchester near Maiden Castle, for instance),

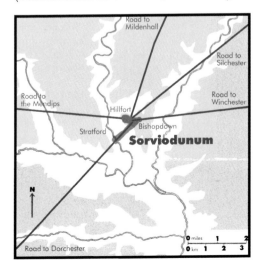

The Salisbury area in the Roman period, showing places mentioned in the text

3

taking over their territories and supplanting them as local capitals. A part of the town of *Soruiodunum* may have existed within the hillfort, but archaeological discoveries suggest that most of it lay outside, dispersed below the east gate (around where the Old Castle Inn now stands) and on the nearby ridge later known as Bishopdown, but most of all in the fields behind present-day Stratford. Its centrepiece was probably a staging-post and lodging establishment for official travellers.

Old Sarum viewed from the west. Some Roman buildings occupied the hillfort, which crowns the skyline. But most of *Sorviodunum* lay below it on the hillside, extending down to and across the river (marked by the line of trees), on either side of the Portway (the diagonal tree-line near the right of the picture), and on Bishopdown (the high ground, extreme right)

Roman rule began to disintegrate during the fourth century, and town life must have become untenable. But the Salisbury area continued to be inhabited and farmed. Cemeteries from these dark centuries have been discovered nearby, at Petersfinger, Charlton, Harnham Hill, and beneath the later city itself, thus indicating where people were buried, if not precisely where they lived. Old Sarum too seems to have reverted (like many other hillforts) to its former role as a refuge; later chronicles record that in the year 552 a battle took place at *Searoburh* which the Saxons won.

Shadowy references such as this – and it may have been no more than a territorial squabble spilling over into a skirmish on or around the hillfort – hint at an unsettled period

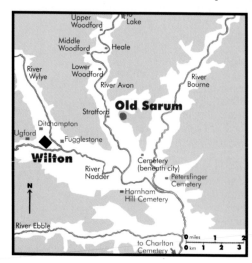

The Salisbury area in the Saxon period, showing places mentioned in the text

of assimilation between native and incomer, Briton and Saxon, about which archaeology and documents tell us little. When the clouds lift we find in place along the river valleys of much of south Wiltshire a pattern of strip territories or farm holdings, each extending from the river up the hillside to the ridge which forms the watershed. These land units, in due course known as tithings, were grouped into larger territories called hundreds, and sometimes named after their central place, such as Downton or Amesbury. The origin of such units and groupings is disputed and uncertain, but in places they seem to go back to Roman or even Iron Age landholdings, and so the hamlets and villages which farmed them in the middle ages may stand in direct line of succession to the native farmsteads at Little Woodbury, Highfield and elsewhere.

The River Avon near Great Durnford, to the north of Old Sarum

Later changes have rendered the partition of the Salisbury area into such tithings obscure, but it is clear that the tradition of a large territory extending up the Avon valley and named after its prominent hillfort continued, or was re-established, during the later Saxon centuries. This territory was now called *Sarisberie*, and must have included a number of small settlements, each with its own tithing. In the Woodford Valley, as the delicious stretch of the sinuous Avon between West Amesbury and Stratford is known, the pattern has survived as present-day hamlets, such as Heale, Lake and the Woodfords; but downstream from Stratford they have been lost beneath the later city.

Five river valleys converge on the Salisbury area. Iron age Old Sarum and Roman *Sorviodunum* were important because they controlled the meeting of ways and river-crossings at the confluence; but from about the ninth century another place emerged as the local centre of government, trade and defence. This was Wilton. Three miles west of modern

The ruined church of St Mary, adjoining Wilton market place, which can be seen beneath the trees beyond

Salisbury, Wilton is a smart little town which, largely because it failed to develop in the middle ages, has retained its Saxon street plan.

Wilton seems to have been promoted in or before the ninth century from the 'farmstead by the River Wylye' implied by its name to the status of a town. It included an enclave containing premises for royal business (remembered now in the name 'Kingsbury' Square), and it possessed a high-status church, or minster (probably on the same site as the ruined St Mary's church). In plan it was roughly square, with four streets meeting at right angles in an open market area at the centre (as they still do).

King Alfred, who reigned from 871 to 899, is credited with stimulating the town's growth in two ways. He included it in a list of strongholds dispersed across his kingdom which local people were to fortify, and then to maintain in readiness to shelter them if attacked. Wilton's new status as a citadel may be reflected in the westward extension of West Street as far as the later St John's Hospital, where a defensive bank was built across the neck of land between the Rivers Nadder and Wylye. Part of it was investigated by archaeologists in 1996. Alfred is supposed also to have richly endowed a nunnery at Wilton (although it is more likely to date from shortly after his death). It lay on the eastern edge of the town, and because it attracted ladies of noble, even royal, birth, its presence contributed to the town's growing wealth and success.

The pre-eminence of Wilton was temporarily checked in 1003, when the town was ravaged by a Danish raiding party. The short-term effect, burnt buildings and spoiled businesses, seems to have been quickly repaired, and the community continued through the eleventh century and into the twelfth to prosper and grow. At its peak it may have had a dozen churches, and it boasted numerous suburbs, such as Ditchampton, Ugford and Fugglestone, which had begun life as its neighbours, riverside farmsteads like itself. But it was the long-term effect of the 1003 raid which would ultimately stunt Wilton's success.

During the mayhem and panic some townspeople decided to seek refuge within the ramparts of Old Sarum, an eventuality for which the old hillfort may deliberately have been kept in repair. They did not all return. Some, moneyers of currency among them, stayed to form a colony, a kind of Wilton outpost, on the hill. Both Wilton and Old Sarum belonged to the crown, although the remainder of the Salisbury estate, which surrounded Old Sarum, had been given by the king to the local diocese (then based at Ramsbury in north Wiltshire) somewhat earlier. This separation suggests that the crown had retained the hillfort because of its potential value to Wilton; and obviously the fledgling colony must have been sanctioned and probably encouraged by the king, who perhaps constituted it into a borough in its own right. If so then Wilton and Old Sarum, both in the same ownership, each with its mint and its market, and only three miles apart, must have co-existed as partners rather than as rivals.

Until 1066 Old Sarum was the weaker partner, and it may have survived as a viable town only through royal support. But the castle-building Normans immediately recognized its strategic potential. A motte was raised and a ditch excavated in the centre of the hillfort, with a bailey or courtyard formed within the eastern half of the Iron Age rampart. Enough building work (initially in wood) had been completed by 1070 for the king to transact business there; later the stone buildings, portions of which survive, were constructed.

Squared masonry replaced the original timber buildings of Old Sarum castle

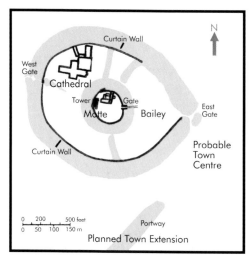

Old Sarum in the Norman period

The surviving footings of Old Sarum cathedral, seen from the castle. East is to the right of the picture

The Norman town of Old Sarum extended outside the hillfort (left) to the area outside its eastern entrance (top, centre), and then down the Portway (centre, line of trees) to the river crossing (bottom right). Part of it probably underlies the present village of Stratford, seen in the middle ground

In 1075 another decision with far-reaching consequences was taken, to move to Old Sarum the seat of the combined diocese of Ramsbury and Sherborne, and build a new cathedral within the western half of the hillfort. The project was overseen by Bishop (eventually Saint) Osmund (1078-99), who turned this unpromising hilltop into a centre of brilliant scholarship and religious innovation. Here was compiled the liturgy known as the *Sarum Use*, which was widely used throughout medieval England and beyond. The first cathedral, completed in 1092, was immediately damaged by lightning and repaired. Osmund's successor, Bishop Roger (1102-39), was also Henry I's chief minister and a powerful politician. As well as enlarging his cathedral to accommodate the thriving religious community, he managed, in about 1130, to acquire control of the castle as well. Once in charge of the entire hillfort he extended the defensive curtain wall almost right around it, effectively gripping the cathedral within the castle's stony embrace. Thus were church and state combined on a windswept Wiltshire hill, just as they were combined in the stormy career of Bishop Roger himself.

Meanwhile the Norman town of Old Sarum, like the Roman *Soruiodunum* a thousand years earlier, was developing beyond the hillfort. Excavations near the Old Castle Inn outside the defences' east gate have discovered roads and

buildings, and a cemetery, of the medieval town. There are references too to churches in this area, and a later map depicts tenement plots extending down the hillside towards the river. This settlement, which flanked the track now known as the Portway and its continuation, part of Stratford's village street, seems to have been a planned regular extension to the original town made during the early twelfth century. Another area of settlement lay west of the hillfort, where a second entrance was cut through the ramparts to give access to the new cathedral precinct.

We call this complex of town, castle and cathedral 'Old' Sarum (*Sarum* is a medieval abbreviation of Salisbury), but to the people living in their riverside farmsteads and hamlets on the bishop's Salisbury estate these developments were newcomers, and their homes were really the 'old' Salisburys. Twelfth-century references to 'Old Salisburys' seem to refer to a group of hamlets now submerged beneath the built-up area of modern Salisbury; the most important of them lay around the present St Martin's church, but

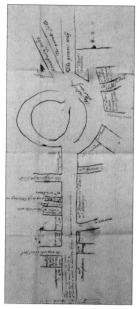

A map of around 1700 showing (for electoral purposes) properties around Old Sarum, and extending south-westwards on either side of the Portway to the river (at the foot of the map) [*courtesy of Salisbury & South Wilts Museum*]

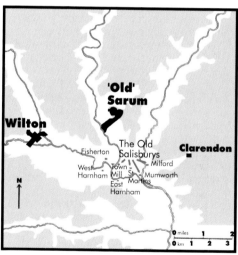

The Salisbury area in the Norman period, showing places mentioned in the text

there were others at Milford and Mumworth (Dairyhouse Bridge on the Southampton Road) to the east, and probably another near the river crossing which became Fisherton Bridge and the Town Mills. The geography of their lanes and fields may have had an important effect on the way in which the later city was laid out.

The troubled anarchy period of the mid-twelfth century did neither of the local towns, Wilton and Old Sarum, any good, and thereafter both seem to have been in irreversible decline. When stability returned to the kingdom the victor, Henry II, spent money on Old Sarum

St Martin's church, marking the site of a village which preceded the present city of Salisbury

Castle, but his main interest in south Wiltshire lay four miles to the south-east, at Clarendon. Here, on a hillside overlooking the Salisbury estate, he converted an old hunting lodge into a magnificent royal palace; frequent visits thereafter by him and his successors ensured that the Salisbury area was never far from the minds of the medieval court.

The twelfth-century bishops of Salisbury may also have had thoughts of improving their premises, but after Roger's death in 1139 little new work was carried out at Old Sarum Cathedral. Instead, the very restricted site in one quadrant of the hillfort (which prevented further enlargement), and the irritation caused by the castle's stranglehold over the clergy's work and worship, suggested another possibility. There would be a new cathedral, and it would be built on land which the bishop already owned and controlled, his estate of Salisbury. And this momentous decision brings us back to the stone-laying ceremony with which we began.

A new beginning: the cathedral spire seen in the distance from the ramparts of Old Sarum

2 THAT ADMIRABLE STRUCTURE

SOMETIMES IT IS EASIER to take a decision than to decide to implement it. In 1194 Herbert Poore was consecrated Bishop of Salisbury, and four years later his brother Richard was appointed Dean. By 1200 not only had the momentous decision to move from Old Sarum been taken, but royal permission had been obtained for the move, the site had been agreed, and building plots for the canons' houses in what would become the Close had been distributed. But, apart perhaps from some planning, groundworks and fundraising, that seems to have been all. No cathedral was begun. Admittedly the reign of King John, from 1199–1216, was a less than auspicious period for such a project, and during the interdict of 1208–13, when most aspects of English church life were suspended on orders from Rome, it would have been impossible. But the main obstacle appears to have been Bishop Herbert himself. He died in 1217 and was replaced by his brother Richard, and this was the signal for the decision, now more than twenty years old, to be implemented at last.

Quite apart from his spiritual and other personal qualities, Richard Poore's achievement should perhaps be seen as that of a successful manager. In order to build a cathedral it was necessary, at one level, to appoint and lead a team of individuals who would be responsible for all the financial, structural and aesthetic aspects of the work. It was essential, too, for the bishop to be able to argue his case with his superiors in both church and state, and obtain their blessing on the work, while at the same time justifying his actions to the clergy and laity of his diocese.

The cost of building the new cathedral was borne initially by the bishop and the members of the chapter. The chapter included the principal diocesan office-holders – the dean,

'Walking Madonna', Elizabeth Frink's sculpture in front of Salisbury Cathedral, which is dedicated to the Virgin Mary

treasurer, precentor and chancellor – and the forty-eight canons, whose income was derived from landholdings known as prebends. The bishop and other officers were all major landowners, and therefore wealthy men, whose estates had grown considerably during the twelfth century. Prebendal incomes varied, and out of them the canons had not only to contribute to the cathedral but also to finance the building of their own houses in the Close.

Two other sources of income were tapped for the cathedral fabric. Donations were sought from everyone from the king downwards, and canons were dispatched on preaching and alms-collecting tours. Henry III in fact made significant benefactions to the work; he stood to gain from the move, of course, because it released for the use of his castle the area occupied at Old Sarum by the old cathedral. The other fund-raising expedient was attempted by Bishop Poore just before he left Salisbury in 1228. This was the canonization of Osmund; and if his petition to the pope had succeeded, the tomb of this venerable figure, whose body was translated to the new cathedral in 1226, might have enjoyed even greater popularity (and therefore income) as a pilgrim shrine than it in fact achieved. Osmund eventually became a saint in 1456, after more than three centuries of veneration at Salisbury, and a new pilgrim shrine was made, probably in the Trinity Chapel.

The design and construction of the cathedral are usually attributed to two men, Elias of Dereham, and Nicholas of Ely. Elias, a highly regarded administrator in the English church with over thirty years' experience by the time that he was made a canon of Salisbury in 1220, seems to have been an expert in supervising major building projects. This expertise was often called upon by other bishops, as well as by the king, and during the 1230s he was involved locally in work at Clarendon Palace and Winchester Castle. Clearly he was interested in and knowledgeable about architecture, but it is

Salisbury Cathedral, vaulting in the Trinity Chapel

impossible to tell how directly he was involved in the design of the new cathedral. Nicholas of Ely (he is sometimes referred to as Robert of Ely, and little is known of his career) appears to have been the master mason responsible for building the cathedral during the early years, and he is the other candidate as the genius behind its design.

New towns on virgin sites were commonplace by the thirteenth century, as we shall see, but new cathedrals were not. In fact Salisbury Cathedral is unique in England in this respect. It is remarkable,

Salisbury Cathedral, looking west from the chancel into the nave

too, for the uniformity and speed with which the basic structure was completed. Such freedom (limited only by the liturgical demands and customs of the Old Sarum chapter) offered Elias or Nicholas – or whoever was responsible for it – an unparalleled opportunity to execute or react to the latest architectural styles, and to introduce fresh ideas about geometry and aesthetics, without having to temper it to adapt to any old-fashioned existing building.

But for the bishop and dean such an innovation presented a couple of problems. First they had to justify the decision, and persuade the authorities that the move was necessary. This they did by reciting a litany of more-or-less plausible complaints about Old Sarum – it was cold and inhospitable, water was scarce, space was limited so that the existing cathedral could not be enlarged, the noise of the wind just over interrupted services and shook the church, the chalk dazzled them, and the castle authorities repeatedly harassed the clergy and their congregation. Second they had to ensure that the work and worship of the cathedral continued during the disruption of the move. To this end a temporary wooden chapel was built at the new site in 1219. In the same year the Old Sarum premises were surrendered to the king, and probably quite soon afterwards the long process of dismantling the old cathedral and reusing materials began. Now there was no turning back.

The stone-laying ceremony in April 1220 was, to use modern jargon, something of a public relations exercise. It was followed by nearly fifty years of continuous building work. The principal material used was a fine-grained limestone, similar to Portland stone, which was quarried and mined from the Tisbury area, twelve miles west of Salisbury. Chilmark stone, as it is known (because the major workings were in the Chilmark ravine west of Tisbury) is the best building stone available in south Wiltshire, and was familiar to the canons from its use in Old Sarum Cathedral, as well as in many parish churches and important houses. Indoors it retains its creamy freshness, but when weathered outside it turns to grey-green. The contrasting dark limestone, known as Purbeck Marble, and used inside for the magnificent slender columns, was mined on the Isle of Purbeck, some thirty-five miles south of Salisbury.

Salisbury Cathedral, plan made by Francis Price and published in 1753

The footings and plinth of the whole cathedral were laid out, and then the work of building commenced at the east end. By September 1225 the first target was achieved – the Trinity Chapel and retrochoir were complete and ready for use. Three altars were consecrated by Bishop Poore, and the Archbishop of Canterbury attended the ceremony and preached. In the next year Osmund's remains, and the tombs of other Old Sarum bishops, were brought to the Trinity Chapel, thus making the new building a focus of pilgrim devotion as well as daily worship. Elias of Dereham lived on for another twenty years, dying a very old man in 1245. Apart from the west front (which he may have designed but which was probably not begun until about 1247) he must have seen substantial portions of the fabric completed, as the whole church was ready for consecration in 1258. The building was not quite finished by this date, however, as work on leading the roof and constructing the chapter house and cloisters (which entailed a change of plan) continued for at least another seven years. A note appended to a document written some fifty years later tells us that the cathedral was completed on 25th March 1266 (the day before Good Friday in that year), and had cost £28,000.

Salisbury Cathedral, view from the nave roof of the chapter house and the east walk of the cloisters

But what we see today is both more and less than what we would have seen in 1266. Less, because a detached bell tower, or campanile, was built within the cathedral graveyard north of the nave. It was surmounted by a spire, and survived until 1790. In 1266 it would have been the tallest building in the Close. This is because the thirteenth-century cathedral had no spire, and its lantern tower extended only to the top of the first stage above the roof-line.

The daring endeavour to raise God's house heavenwards has left no documentary evidence, and the date of the spire can be conjectured only on stylistic and comparative evidence. The period between 1300 and 1330 is now considered the most likely. It was the time when the medieval church reached the pinnacle of its wealth, before the profound demographic and social changes of the fourteenth century, including the Black Death in 1348-9, began to reduce the income from its agricultural estates. Spires were then in fashion, and many which have now fallen were added to existing church towers. At Salisbury this meant raising and buttressing the tower to receive a stone spire – revolutionary for its time, since spires were usually of wood – which would double the total height of the building. The spire is in fact virtually the same height as the tower on which it stands – each are

Salisbury Cathedral, the bell tower demolished in 1790

200 feet (61 metres) – and this is also the width of the transepts.

At 404 feet (123 metres) Salisbury Cathedral has the tallest medieval spire in England (as everyone seems to know), but in the fourteenth century this was by no means the case. Not only was Salisbury not the tallest in England, it was not even the tallest in Wiltshire. Supposedly Malmesbury Abbey's spire, which fell in about 1500, was taller, and occupied a far more dominant site in relation to its surrounding countryside. Of cathedral spires Lincoln's central tower was raised in 1307 to carry a spire some 525 feet high. It blew down in 1548, thirteen years before the spire of Old St Paul's in London, which had been almost its equal. Of surviving spires Salisbury is often compared with St Mary Redcliffe in Bristol, with which it is contemporary (although rebuilt in the nineteenth century), and which had belonged to the Salisbury chapter.

With the capstone securely on top of the spire Salisbury's medieval cathedral was complete. The concern of later generations of clergy and masons right up to the present day has been to monitor, preserve and restore. In addition to buttressing added to support the weight of the spire at the time of its construction, the fifteenth century saw bracing arches inserted to strengthen the crossing, and following a survey by Sir Christopher Wren in 1669, reinforcements were made to the tower. Radical changes were inflicted on the cathedral interior by the architect James Wyatt during the years following 1789. They involved the destruction or resiting of many medieval accretions and, although they met with the approval of most clergy and some scholars at the time, they were bitterly criticized and, where possible, ameliorated by the Victorians.

'Purity' is the concept which architectural historians have bandied about when considering Salisbury Cathedral, from the time of Wyatt and then the Victorians onwards. From start to finish the work (apart from the spire) was built in about fifty years, and in a single architectural style. Nothing was there before, and, apart from the spire added a few decades later, nothing too drastic has happened to it since. This is Salisbury's unique distinction among English medieval cathedrals. But the long-held assumptions that Salisbury Cathedral is the pure standard set by an unfettered architectural genius, and the supreme achievement in a particular style, have recently been called into question. There are strong echoes of Old Sarum in New Sarum Cathedral, particularly in the treatment of the chancel and

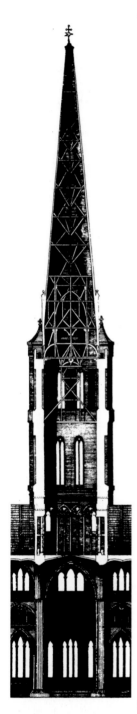

Salisbury Cathedral tower and spire, cutaway elevation made by Francis Price and published in 1753

east end. There are many references in the design to other recent or contemporary cathedral building campaigns in England and France, and in some ways Salisbury is reactionary more than trendsetting. Furthermore, although it can be shown that well-known principles of masonic geometry were employed, the units of measurement, as well as many of the architectural details, are not consistent throughout the building.

The style adopted, which is referred to now as Early English or first Gothic, was introduced from France towards the end of the twelfth century, and its first major use was in the rebuilding after a fire of the choir of Canterbury Cathedral between 1175 and 1184. It quickly became the vogue, and was used for cathedral rebuildings at Lincoln, Winchester and elsewhere. But Salisbury's most important antecedent was Wells, where rebuilding the cathedral in Early English style began about 1180 and continued until about 1260. The builders of Wells, like those of Salisbury, started from the east end and worked westwards. The nave was reached by about 1200 and the west front by about 1230, so they were some thirty years ahead of their Salisbury counterparts. The details and dimensions of the two buildings are quite different, but both were built within the same architectural tradition. The contrast is well seen by comparing their two west fronts, both solid walls of statuary designed as display cabinets for the hierarchical medieval system of saints and Biblical worthies, and highlit in the middle ages with brightly coloured paints. The medium is the same, the message is the same (even though at Salisbury the full complement of statues was never achieved), but the artistic effect achieved by each is quite individual.

Salisbury, like Wells, was a secular cathedral, one of nine English medieval cathedrals which were not also monasteries, but relied for their organization and worship on a chapter of 'secular' canons. This fact affected the design of the cathedral itself, in that the cloisters had a purely liturgical or processional function, and did not form a quadrangle surrounded by the refectory, dormitory and other conventual buildings of an abbey. But a more important consideration for the cathedral

Salisbury Cathedral, visible are part of a strainer arch and buttresing added to the crossing to support the weight of the spire

Salisbury Cathedral, the west front

Salisbury Cathedral, the south and west walks of the cloisters

planners was where the bishop, the senior office-holders and the forty-eight canons would live. It was the need to provide for them that created the close of houses which surround the cathedral.

Salisbury Close today is an assembly of distinguished houses of many architectural periods and styles. Taking its lead from showpieces such as Malmesbury House, Mompesson House and Arundells, it exudes an

Salisbury Cathedral Close, the principal buildings

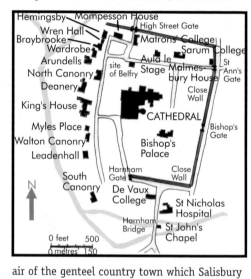

Elias of Dereham's Leadenhall, the model for the canon's houses, photographed in a ruinous state before it was demolished in 1915

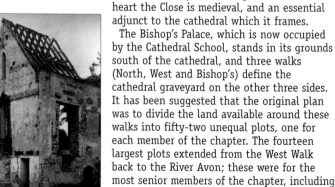

air of the genteel country town which Salisbury was to become in the eighteenth century, and which we shall explore in chapter six. But at heart the Close is medieval, and an essential adjunct to the cathedral which it frames.

The Bishop's Palace, which is now occupied by the Cathedral School, stands in its grounds south of the cathedral, and three walks (North, West and Bishop's) define the cathedral graveyard on the other three sides. It has been suggested that the original plan was to divide the land available around these walks into fifty-two unequal plots, one for each member of the chapter. The fourteen largest plots extended from the West Walk back to the River Avon; these were for the most senior members of the chapter, including the dean, whose hall (now known as the Medieval Hall) still stands, concealed behind later buildings, opposite the cathedral's west front. One of these fourteen, called Leadenhall, was begun by Elias of Dereham in 1221 as his own house, but also as a model for the other canons to emulate. The lesser chapter members were expected to build their houses on smaller plots abutting the North and Bishop's (east) Walks. Such an arrangement seems to have been envisaged long before the cathedral was begun, by about 1199, when the plots were actually allotted individually to the canons.

The plan when implemented soon ran into difficulties. Each canon was expected to build a house at his own expense, so that he could accommodate his vicar choral (who deputized for him at cathedral services) and other staff, and also in order to provide the hospitality expected of him. But by 1222 many canons appear not to have started building, and it is likely that for many the financial commitment proved too daunting. In the event most canons resided only intermittently, and the successors of some of those who had built, on a suitably lavish scale, found the burden of upkeep too great. From the fourteenth century most houses in the Close had become the corporate property of the dean and chapter, or belonged to the bishop, and they were then allocated to canons according to seniority and choice. But fewer canons chose to, or could afford to, reside in the Close, and by the end of the middle ages houses were being let to laymen who had no involvement in the business of the cathedral. Only seven properties remained as canons' residences, and most of these were rebuilt during the sixteenth century. Some properties were badly treated during the civil war and commonwealth period, so that the restoration of

The Bishop's Palace, (now the Cathedral School) in the Close

The Walton Canonry, a house of about 1720 on the site of a medieval canonry

the later seventeenth century saw considerable rebuilding, especially by lay gentry who chose to establish their family seats in the Close. The Matrons' College also dates from this period, and several houses were converted for use as schools.

Despite the vicissitudes of Close life and the changing fortunes of its houses, many of the property boundaries established in the thirteenth century (and perhaps earmarked before 1200) have survived, and a number of houses have preserved, overtly or concealed, portions of their medieval architecture. They include Aula Le Stage, Arundells, the King's House (formerly the prebendal house of Sherborne Abbey, and now Salisbury and South Wiltshire Museum), the Old Deanery (now called the Medieval Hall), Hemingsby and the North Canonry, as well as parts of the Bishop's Palace.

One other very prominent feature of the medieval Close remains to be mentioned. In 1317 it was granted the right of sanctuary, and in 1327 licence was obtained to build a defensive wall around it. Four years later the king agreed to allow the dean and chapter to use stone from Old Sarum Cathedral for this purpose (they had in fact been using the old cathedral as a quarry for many years), and the wall was begun. Carved stones and mason's

Aula le Stage ('the tower house'), a well documented medieval canonry which was several times remodelled, notably during the sixteenth century

marks may still be spotted in many places along the Exeter Street face of the surviving Close wall. The battlemented wall was built around all four sides of the Close, although St Nicholas's Hospital and other buildings at the Close's southern edge were left outside, and almost all the western wall, between the Close and the River Avon, was later demolished. Contemporary

The Matron's College, one of the showpieces of the seventeenth-century architectural renewal of the Close

with the wall are the three gates which admit access to the Close, the High Street, Harnham and St Ann's Gates, although part of the High Street Gate was rebuilt during the fifteenth century. A fourth gate was built after 1377 as a private access to the Bishop's Palace from Exeter Street.

The medieval diocese of Salisbury encompassed the three counties of Wiltshire, Berkshire and Dorset. When the bishop, the dean and the canons met in their cathedral chapter house they must have been an awesome sight. For there, surrounded by the magnificent architecture of their own making, sat a body of men who not only wielded enormous power over the spiritual lives of all the inhabitants of a sizeable portion of southern England; they also, as individual landowners, were the direct beneficiaries of the labours of many of those

High Street Gate,
looking from the
city into the Close

inhabitants, scattered in their acres from
Windsor to Lyme. Much of the wealth thus
created had enabled Salisbury Cathedral and
Close to be built and to flourish. And because
clergy and their servants, like anyone else,
required food and clothing, and a range of other
goods and services, a flourishing community
within the Close walls meant a flourishing town
of tradesmen outside.

3 BRAVE NEW CITY

TOWN PLANNING and the creation of new towns, overspill areas and suburbs are such familiar and apparently modern concepts in the twentieth century, that it is easy to overlook the obvious fact that all towns were new once. Many quaint and picturesque old places began life as speculative new towns laid out by a medieval town planner, and the more successful were extended, reorientated and developed suburbs, as well as suffering from the familiar urban problems of overcrowding, unhealthy living conditions and civil disorder. Wilton was a town planned and extended in the Saxon period, and the urban portions of Old Sarum were created, probably in stages, between the tenth and twelfth centuries. The difference between Saxon or medieval new towns, and those of the present day, is not one of concept but of scale. Even the largest medieval town had a population of only a few thousand, and most were no bigger than modern villages. Nearly 200 entirely new towns in England have been identified which were established between 1066 and 1300, and countless more were enlarged or extended to accommodate the country's growing population and economic vigour.

Against this background the idea of building a town on the rural Salisbury estate next to the new cathedral seems unremarkable, in fact almost inevitable. Some kind of settlement would have been necessary, if only to house the workforce and feed the clergy. But in fact the bishop had a more ambitious plan. He was no

This eighteenth-century view of Salisbury from the north-west depicts the city dwarfed by its cathedral, and depicts also the bell tower (immediately right of the cathedral) and to its right the prominent church towers of St Thomas, St Edmund and St Clement (Fisherton). Winchester Gate, the city's principal entrance from the east, is shown above the team of horses drawing the coach.

Salisbury's medieval street plan, showing places mentioned in the text

doubt aware of what had been done at Lichfield in Staffordshire a century earlier. There the old Saxon cathedral had been rebuilt during the 1120s and 1130s, and a new town, with its own church, market place and grid of streets had been laid out alongside the cathedral close. He may also have been familiar with Bury St Edmunds in Suffolk, which between 1066 and 1086 had doubled its population, and had developed an extensive rectilinear plan of streets outside the gates of the important abbey. He knew of course that Devizes (which belonged to him) was a town planned and established by one of his predecessors as bishop of Salisbury. And he must have been uncomfortably conscious of the town-building activities of his neighbour, the bishop of Winchester, which had included since 1200 speculative developments at Hindon and Downton in Wiltshire, as well as various new towns in Hampshire.

Having begun his cathedral in the meadow beside the way from Old Sarum to Aegel's Ford, and having laid out the plots for the canons' houses within the sweep of the river, Bishop Poore was somewhat constrained in the choice of site for his new town. The river to south and west defined not only the cathedral close but also the limit of his Salisbury estate. Beyond, in Fisherton and Harnham, the land belonged to others, and so was not available to him. To the east lay Bugmore (now the Greyfriars area and the ring road), which was then poorly drained marshland unsuitable for much development. North of Bugmore there was already a village on the rising ground, with its own church (St Martin's) and village street (now St Martin's Church Street).

North of the close, along the road to Old Sarum (now Castle Street), the ground was flat for the first half-mile, and was intersected by another road which descended Milford Hill further east and made its way westwards to a river crossing on the site of the present Fisherton Bridge. Near this crossing stood the bishop's watermill, and around it were perhaps a few houses. All this flat land, from the river to the slopes of Milford Hill, we may assume to have formed part of the meadows and arable fields of the bishop's estate. Here, he must have decided, was the only suitable site for his new town.

The Town Mill, beside Fisherton Bridge, which occupies the site of a watermill belonging to the bishop before his new city was established

It was, in fact, an excellent site. Level, spacious, and with a good water supply, it also enjoyed easy access by important roads from north and east, and by river-crossings to other roads from south and west. Building work on and around the cathedral was set to continue for many years, offering ample opportunities for employment and scope for providing in the new town what would now be called service industries. To the perhaps disillusioned inhabitants of the awkward and rambling settlement spilling from its windswept, waterless hillside at Old Sarum the new town must have seemed like the promised land, and so from there and from all the surrounding countryside people flocked down the road to make the most of it.

With hindsight it is easy to list these reasons why New Salisbury (as the bishop called his city) was an instant success. But in 1220 the decisions taken must have combined elements of pious devotion and good luck, as well as shrewd business sense. There are in fact indications (in the form of early ward boundaries and the street layout itself) that the new city was planned and built in two stages. An initial plan, to develop land as far north as the east-west road (which was possibly also a field boundary), was quickly revised as the project's popularity became apparent, and a more ambitious grid of streets and a spacious market place were laid out beyond.

The houses of the close, as we have seen, were laid out around three walks, and the north walk continued eastwards towards St Martin's church and village. Behind the houses of the north walk was (and is) a parallel boundary line, which marks the northern limit of the close, and was from an early date defined by a deep watercourse, the Close Ditch. Beyond it, and also parallel with it at one tenement's depth, was laid out a long, straight street, which extends from a river-crossing at its western end (now Crane Bridge) to the village street of St Martin's in the east (the junction now lies beneath the ring road). This, traditionally the first street to be built, was appropriately known along its whole length as 'New Street'; part of it has retained this original name.

The Close Ditch turned southwards to skirt and define the eastern limit of the close, and alongside it a second new street, now Exeter

The first new street to be laid out in the city is traditionally believed to have extended from the far end of St Martin's Church Street, now a quiet backwater to the east of the city (above), to Crane Bridge in the west (right), where the River Avon marks the limit of the bishop's territory

Street, was built. With a deflection where it met the north walk, this street was continued northwards across the fields in the direction of Old Sarum. This line now has various names, including Endless Street, but it was originally known as 'High Street' along its whole length. It must have carried north—south traffic from Old Sarum to Aegel's Ford, as a kind of by-pass to avoid the cathedral and close. Another deep watercourse was also dug, which drew water from the Avon just below the bishop's mill, and ran eastwards along what is now the street called New Canal, until rising ground forced it to turn south and make its way across Bugmore back to the river.

This then seems to have been the first town plan. The two new streets, which met at right angles, formed the backbone of a settlement which extended from St Martin's village in the south-east to the bishop's mill and river-crossing in the north-west, and which was drained and defined along much of its northern and southern edges by the two large watercourses. But if this was the original scheme then the new city quickly outgrew it. Probably by 1230, ten years after the stone-laying ceremony, much more ambitious plans were afoot.

A large, roughly rectangular area, extending from the river in the west to the so-called 'High Street' (now Queen Street) in the east, and from the Town Ditch (New Canal) in the south to Blue Boar Row in the north, was left open as the city's market place. This piece of town planning was probably in response to the securing in 1227 of a royal charter granting market and other rights. Although today's market place seems large it originally covered a much greater area still, which has subsequently been encroached upon by shops. The first encroachment, in fact, took place more or less immediately, with the building during the 1230s of a chapel on its western side. Hardly surprisingly, this chapel was dedicated to St Thomas Becket, who had been murdered some sixty years earlier, in 1170, and whose cult was enjoying enormous popularity; in the very year of Salisbury's birthday, 1220, his bones had been transferred into a special shrine within

Catherine Street, looking south to St John's Street, part of the original 'High Street' line. The traffic lights at which the cars are waiting marks the 'New Street' east–west line, so this may have been the first new cross-roads of the thirteenth-century city

This 1930s aerial photograph clearly shows how St Thomas's church, largely rebuilt in the fifteenth century, has been crowded with rows of small shops, which have infilled the western and southern parts of the formerly much larger open market place

27

Canterbury Cathedral. The chapel in Salisbury market place had become by 1246 the first new parish church of the city.

North and east of the market place a grid of streets was laid out, parallel or at right angles to those features which had already been established. The grid is not entirely regular. This is partly because the earlier features themselves, Castle Street and Endless Street, the New Canal and the market place, are themselves not regular. But there was another reason too. One of Old Sarum's problems had been its lack of a convenient water supply. Here in New Sarum, because the site was level and close to the river, the town planners decided that it would be possible to provide the city with a supply of running water. A system of watercourses was devised which could draw water from the Avon (or rather from the bishop's mill leat next to it), and channel it along many of the new streets as far as Bugmore, where it rejoined the river (near the present Salisbury College).

To do this smoothly and effectively some of the streets, such as St Edmund's Church Street and Gigant Street, have to bend slightly to respect the contours. These watercourses became a notable feature of Salisbury, and visitors often commented on them. Until about 1737 they were wide and ran down the middle of streets, giving Salisbury its sobriquet, 'the English Venice'. But they have subsequently been blamed for much of the city's poor public health record. After 1737 they were confined within brick channels along the roadsides, and after contributing to a cholera epidemic in 1849 they were removed as a health hazard, despite prolonged opposition from vested interests.

Roman towns employed grid plans, and the resulting divisions were called in Latin [i]insulae[r], 'islands'. Gridded American cities call them blocks. In Salisbury they are called chequers, and their individual names are derived from prominent buildings, such as inns, or from important owners. Thus we have Antelope Chequer, Three Swans Chequer, Swayne's Chequer, and many others — no fewer than 21 named chequers altogether. Salisbury is not the only new medieval city to have a grid of streets. Bury St Edmunds has already been mentioned, and other good examples are Ludlow in Shropshire and New Winchelsea in Sussex. Many more modest examples, with just a few blocks or chequers, have also survived.

A chequer pattern, even if it was not entirely rectilinear, made it easier to divide up a city into individual properties, which were known as burgage tenements. Bishop Poore in

This nineteenth-century engraving of Minster Street shows an open watercourse flowing along the roadside. Until 1737 such 'canals' had been much wider and more prominent

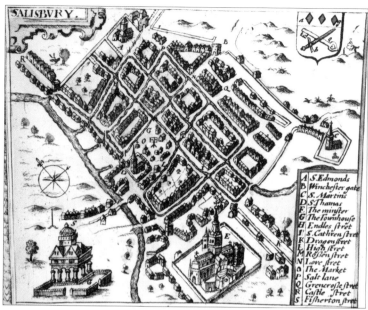

The key on the map reads:

A S.Edmonds
B Winchester gate
C S. Martins
D S.Thomas
E The minster
G TheTownhouse
H Endles ſtret
I S.Cathren ſtret
K Dragon ſtret
L High ſtret
M Rosſien ſtret
N Love ſtret
O The Market
P Salt lane
Q Grencroſle ſtret
R Caſtle ſtret
S Fiſherton ſtret

1225 had established a standard size of burgage, approximately 35 metres long by 15 metres wide, and the north—south streets in the eastern part of the city run about 70 metres, or two burgage lengths, apart. Although all land in the city remained the bishop's property, and he derived a fixed annual rent from each of his burgage tenants, the individual tenements could change hands, could be built on in a variety of ways, and could be subdivided or combined. Many of the best commercial sites, such as those fronting the market place or at corners, were from an early date divided up in ingenious ways, and their architectural and occupational history has become very complicated. In the backstreets of the eastern chequers, however, property boundaries were less vulnerable to change, and a few have survived to the present day, even though the buildings on them may have been replaced several times.

A measure of the city's success during its first fifty years may be seen in a document of 1269, in which a new parish was created, and all the parish boundaries were described. Housing seems by then to have extended over almost all the planned area, and continued a little way up Castle Street beyond the intended city limit. Until 1269 Salisbury was served by the cathedral and two parish churches, the old St Martin's, and the new St Thomas's. But by 1264 work had begun on another, larger church in the north-eastern corner of the planned city. Like St Thomas's this was dedicated to a 'modern' saint, St Edmund of Abingdon. He had been treasurer of Salisbury Cathedral during the early years of

John Speed's plan of Salisbury in 1610, although not entirely accurate, shows well the chequers into which the city was divided by its street plan. Notice the watercourses and also the lack of suburbs, apart from Fisherton Street (to the left) and Castle Street (top left). St Martin's church stands isolated on the right of the plan

St Edmund's Church served the poorer northern and eastern chequers of medieval Salisbury and, until its tower fell demolishing much of the nave in 1653, it was roughly twice as large as the existing building, which is now an arts centre

Craddock House and Friary Court, on or close to the site of the Franciscan friary

Harnham Bridge, originally built in about 1244, offered travellers to the west country a convenient crossing of the south Wiltshire river system – and funnelled them through the new city, in preference to its rival, Wilton

its building, from 1222 to 1234, and had then been appointed archbishop of Canterbury. He was canonised during the 1240s, soon after his death.

Medieval St Edmund's was much larger than the fragment which survives today as an arts centre; about half of it was demolished after its tower collapsed in 1653. It was a collegiate church, which meant that a permanent community of clergymen was attached to it, rather like a small monastery, and they served the spiritual needs of both St Edmund's and St Martin's parishes. The present council offices at Bourne Hill are on the site of these priests' domestic quarters. Other religious communities, too, were attracted to settle in the growing city. Franciscan friars came to Salisbury in about 1230, possibly at Bishop Poore's invitation, and built premises on the edge of Bugmore, in an area which is still known as the Greyfriars. Fifty years later the Dominican or black friars transferred their attention from Wilton to Salisbury, and built a friary just outside the city on the northern side of Fisherton Street, close to the bridge.

This was in 1281, and their decision to move was a clear sign that Salisbury was gaining the ascendancy over its long-established rival,

Wilton. One reason for this, which was recognised as long ago as the sixteenth century, was a project undertaken by Bishop Poore's successor, Robert Bingham, in about 1244. Bishop Bingham built a bridge, Ayleswade or Harnham Bridge, across the River Avon south of the cathedral close and not far from Aegel's Ford. The effect of this was to entice long-distance travellers heading across south Wiltshire away from their established route past Old Sarum and over a river crossing close to the present Bull Bridge in Wilton, and to take them through Salisbury instead. To maintain the new bridge, and to care for travellers using it, he endowed St John's Chapel on the little island

which divides the river's two channels at this point, and he reconstituted a hospital nearby, which was dedicated to St Nicholas. In 1262 a later bishop established a hostel for students on a site next to the hospital. This was known as De Vaux College, or the House of the Valley of Scholars, and the name was derived from a kind of 'alternative' university established in the Auvergne in France. The hostel catered for students who had arrived in Salisbury after being dispersed from Oxford in 1238 and again in 1264-78, and it had the makings of a university in its own right.

In little more than sixty years, 1220-1280, Bishop Poore's New Salisbury had graduated from

Two important medieval buildings between the Close and Harnham Bridge, depicted before Victorian alterations. St Nicholas's Hospital (above), and De Vaux College (below)

A surviving portion of
the city's medieval
ramparts, at Bourne
Hill

an act of faith to an important city, with busy
streets and markets, churches and chapels, and a
centre of learning, religion and trade. Thereafter
the town plan needed very little modification.
Half-heartedly, and more as a boundary than as
a defence, an earthen bank was constructed to
define the city's limits on its northern and
eastern sides. Across the bridges, in Fisherton
and in Harnham, suburbs developed along the
main roads. And gradually the market place
began to fill up with rows of buildings, as we are
about to discover. But in essence Salisbury's
medieval plan was complete by 1280, and it was
destined to remain virtually unaltered until the
nineteenth century.

4 INCOME AND INCOMERS

A SURVIVING LIST of Salisbury taxpayers in 1332 includes the names of John and Stephen de Pultone. Both lived somewhere in Market Ward, therefore close to the market place or along Castle Street, and John's tax assessment implies that he was among the fifty wealthiest inhabitants of the city. Their name suggests that either they themselves, or perhaps a father or grandfather, had arrived in Salisbury from a place called Poulton. There is such a place on the outskirts of Marlborough, about thirty miles away, and another near Cirencester, rather further. Of the 170 inhabitants assessed for tax in 1332 at least half had names of this type, many referring to towns and villages within a day's walk of Salisbury, but others to more distant places, including Bristol, Taunton and London.

Some sixty-five years and three generations later another tax list records Robert Polton, a barber-surgeon, living in Market Ward. Nearby, perhaps next-door, was a fuller of cloth, and at least five dyers lived in the vicinity. Like Robert several of his neighbours had names derived from places, including Tisbury, Winterslow, Yeovil and Lavington. Whether or not Robert was descended from the John or Stephen of 1332 it is impossible to say. Nor can we tell whether or when the ancestors of his neighbour, John Wynterslewe, moved into Salisbury from the nearby village of Winterslow.

But it is from lists of individuals such as these that it is possible to gain some idea of Salisbury's ups and downs since the halcyon days of the thirteenth century. They suggest that by 1332 so many tradesmen and entrepreneurs like the de Pultones had sought their fortunes in

A Salisbury tax list of about 1399. This is part of Market ward, and the names of householders are probably arranged in the same order as their houses. Robert Polton, barber, is nine names up from the bottom of this extract

33

Salisbury that it had become the tenth wealthiest city in England. In 1377 its population probably exceeded 5,000, and took it to seventh in the league table of English cities; of places artificially created during the middle ages it was the most successful of all. By about 1500, when Salisbury probably reached its medieval peak, it may have had about 8,000 inhabitants, and was only surpassed in southern England by London, Bristol and Exeter. Thereafter its population declined slightly, against a background of steadily rising totals both for England as a whole and for other large towns.

Salisbury's medieval achievement is the more remarkable when it is set against the national picture. The thirteenth century was a period of growth, with the population in the countryside rising faster than could be supported by the agricultural economy of the villages. It was not surprising, therefore, that places like Poulton might see its young men and women departing for a new life in the expanding towns. But after 1300 disease, famine and a worsening climate depopulated town and countryside alike. Many villages shrank to isolated hamlets or farms, or disappeared altogether, including several (Redenham, Baverstock and Syrencot, for example) from which prominent emigrés to Salisbury had taken their surnames. Many towns became no larger than villages – and yet Salisbury continued to grow for another two centuries.

Three explanations may be offered for this paradox. First there was the cathedral, which meant employment for builders and administrators, as we have seen, and gave local

Salisbury has always been a magnet for visitors, whether on business or as pilgrims to the cathedral. This nineteenth-century engraving depicts Castle Street, the city's main approach from the north

traders and craftsmen opportunities to sell their products, both to the resident and visiting churchmen and to the pilgrims. Alongside this ecclesiastical source of wealth may be bracketed its secular neighbour, the royal palace at Clarendon, which at times also brought money and moneyed people into the Salisbury area. Second, and hinted at in the mention of the fullers and dyers who lived in Market Ward, was the woollen manufacturing industry, and this will be the subject of our next chapter. The third leg of this metaphorical three-legged stool was the buoyancy and vitality of Salisbury's market.

The landowners — including bishops — who built medieval towns expected to derive income from them in two principal ways: from the rents paid by their inhabitants, and from the tolls and fines levied at their markets. A successful market was paramount, because without it no-one would come to live in the town, and so no-one would pay rent. Many attempts to found towns failed because they were too close to established market centres with which they could not compete. Markets at Downton and Amesbury, both within eight miles of Salisbury, never became significant. Conversely a new market town might entice trade away from its old-established neighbours; Salisbury's success proved the downfall of the markets at Wilton and Old Sarum.

Interim permission to hold a market at Salisbury had been secured by the bishop from the king as early as 1219, and this was several times renewed until a royal charter was obtained in 1227. This authorised a market every Tuesday and a ten-day fair during each August. Wilton was not pleased, especially if its allegation, made in 1240, was true, that markets were being held daily in the new city, to the detriment of its own trade. Wilton's bailiffs apparently resorted to force, and compelled traders on their way to Salisbury to sell in Wilton market place instead. But complaints and intimidation could not alter the economic reality, and even the crown's influence and interest in support of Wilton failed to stifle Salisbury's vigour. A compromise in 1315 resolved that Salisbury should have a second market day, Saturday, but should leave the other days for Wilton and Old Sarum. The pattern of weekly markets in Salisbury on Tuesday and Saturday has continued ever since.

Markets were as much a part of ordinary urban life in the middle ages as supermarkets are today, necessary for the inhabitants both of the town itself and of its surrounding countryside. But apart from its day-to-day shopping function an important market such as

Wilton market place, from a plan of around 1568. The gardens and empty plots bordering the square suggest a market long in decline

The western edge of the present market place is all infilling around St Thomas's church (left) and the site of the cheese cross (near the market hall façade (right)

Salisbury's had regional importance, a place where bargains might be struck between cloth factors, graziers or corn dealers. In this respect Salisbury's success affected the fortunes of other large towns, such as Winchester, Southampton and Shaftesbury, which lay outside its immediate ambit.

The same regional significance was invested in Salisbury's fairs, great annual gatherings for trade in agricultural produce, livestock, cloth and luxuries. At the height of the city's prosperity, around 1500, five fairs seem to have been held each year, in January (Epiphany), March (Lady Day), Whitsun, September/October (Michaelmas) and November (St Edmund's Day). The Greencroft, an open area at the city's eastern limits, was used for some of these fairs, but the Whitsun fair took place in the Close, and St Edmund's fair was held around the churchyard of St Edmund's Church. The fairs dwindled in the nineteenth century and lost their agricultural importance. Now only the Michaelmas fair survives, and purely as a pleasure fair; for a week each autumn the market place is full of the razzmatazz of dodgems, candy floss and roundabouts.

Today's market place, quite large enough to lose children and companions in on market day, covers less than half the area originally allotted to it in the thirteenth century. This, as we have seen, extended south to the present New Canal

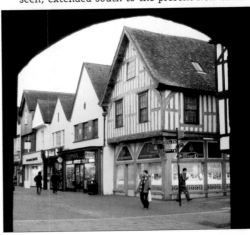

The corner of Butcher Row and the former Ironmonger Row, seen from the Poultry Cross

and west to the river. St Thomas's Church was the first of many encroachments, as regular traders in particular commodities gave permanence to their pitches by erecting rows of buildings. Market infill, as this process of encroachment is known, occurred commonly in successful towns in the middle ages. In Salisbury we still have Butcher Row and Fish Row, Ox Row and Oatmeal Row, and there are medieval references to several others.

Purveyors of foodstuffs and household goods clustered around St Thomas's churchyard and the first market cross, which occupied the site of the present Poultry Cross. Here were rows and shops occupied by ironmongers, bakers, cooks and shoemakers, and sellers of pots and bottles,

The northern edge of the market place, Blue Boar Row, is in its original position. A medieval building, the Boar, survives within the much later architecture of the department store (right)

Late medieval houses in Minster Street, the successors of market stalls which became permanent fixtures

greengrocery, poultry, fish and meat. In the fifteenth century the greengrocery and dairy products were moved to the area between St Thomas's Church and Castle Street, which is still known as the Cheesemarket, and a cheese cross was erected there; at the same period Salisbury's one surviving cross acquired its present name, the Poultry Cross.

The Poultry Cross as it appeared until the 1850s (right), when the surrounding low wall was removed and the elaborate super-structure added (below)

This remote world of medieval shopping is brought rather closer to us by the work of archaeologists and collectors. When new sewers were being laid in the 1850s to replace the open watercourses the workmen kept finding keys and spoons, buckles, ornaments and other metalwork which had been lost or thrown away in the mud of the channels during the middle ages. Well over a thousand such items were collected to form in 1860 the original nucleus of the present Salisbury and South Wiltshire Museum. Many, we can assume, were made in the city by Salisbury craftsmen, and sold in the market place. And so a small fraction of the contents of the iron-monger's stock in trade, as well as examples of the shoemaker's tools, the buckles he sewed to the shoes, even the frame of his customer's purse and the door-key once safe inside it — all these can now be seen in the museum's drainage collection.

Also in the museum are examples of the types of cooking pot, jugs and other domestic pottery which, we may assume, were supplied to the traders in 'pot row' by medieval potters from their kilns at Laverstock, just outside the city. Nine kilns were investigated between 1955 and 1963, and the excavations revealed details of the working methods and products of an industry which found a ready market in the new city during the thirteenth century. Similarly an excavation carried out in the eastern chequers next to Guilder Lane in 1972 uncovered the remains of the workshop of a brazier and bellfounder, John Barbur. His business, which included making copper cooking utensils for the Salisbury market as well as church bells, brought him prosperity and left his widow, when he died in 1404, a wealthy woman.

Since the 1980s archaeological excavations in advance of new buildings in the city centre have brought evidence to light about the diet and lifestyle of our medieval ancestors, especially in the poorer eastern chequers, such

as Gigant Street and Brown Street. Archaeology
can even tell us how the butchers in Butcher
Row went about their business. A study of the
animal bones recovered from medieval domestic
sites excavated in Salisbury between 1985 and
1988 identified the various butchering tech-
niques – splitting, chopping, cutting and sawing
– used in preparing joints of beef, mutton and
pork. Allied to this a long-running project at
Salisbury Museum to catalogue and describe its
entire medieval collection of artefacts is (2004)
nearing completion, so that soon we shall have
a much clearer notion of everyday life in the
city six or seven centuries ago.

Satisfying the domestic needs of the
Salisbury citizen was only one of the functions
of the market place. Surplus corn and other
agricultural produce was carted into market by
manorial bailiffs and tenants for their lords from
all over the city's extensive hinterland. This, by
the later middle ages seems to have included the
whole of south Wiltshire, and adjacent parts of
Hampshire and Dorset. The corn market was
apparently held along the northern side of the
market place, facing what is now called Blue
Boar Row. A cattle market may also have been
held in the market place during the early years,
as it certainly was in the nineteenth century,
but by 1428 cattle were sold near Barnard's
Cross. This stood in the south-eastern chequers,
on the way to St Martin's. Wool, in all the stages
of manufacture from fleece to finished cloth,
was the concern of the eastern side of the
market place, fronting what is now Queen
Street. There are medieval references to a cross
here, and to a building called the yarn market.

What else might one expect to find on sale
in a flourishing medieval city? The citizens
needed fuel for their hearths, and there seems
to have been a wood market (and later a coal
market) held in the area of New Canal. Some
street names appear to refer to essential or
desirable commodities on sale there, such as Salt
Lane, Silver Street and Wineman Street (now
Winchester Street); Love Lane may also fall into
this category. But such names sometimes refer
rather to the surname of a family who lived
there — the Chipper family, whose name
appropriately means 'market-trader', were living
in the area of Chipper Lane, next to the market
place, by 1306.

Then there were the city inns and alehouses.
Blue Boar Row, which forms the northern side of
the market place, is, like many of the chequers,
named after an inn. One portion of the Boar
Inn, as it was known in the fifteenth century,
survives as the restaurant buried deep within
Debenham's department store. It was built in

Alley leading from the
Cheesemarket to St
Thomas's church and
square. The citizens'
first council office
occupied the plot on
the left in the later
middle ages

1444, and the written agreement between client and builder has survived, setting out the dimensions and materials to be used. The Queen Street frontage of the market place now includes a modern shopping mall, which retains elements, including a crooked staircase, of a large courtyard inn, the Plume of Feathers. Other medieval buildings around the market place still function as inns, including the Haunch of Venison and the Chough, but this may not have been their original function. The names of many medieval inns in the city are recorded in documents; in fact it appears that a large proportion of city centre tenements have at one time or other been licensed premises. The High Street, in particular, was lined with large medieval inns which catered for travellers and pilgrims. The facade and part of the George Inn

Cross Keys Chequer, a 1970s reconstruction of the yard of the medieval Plume of Feathers Inn (right), with its crooked staircase to a first-floor gallery (above)

has been retained. Fisherton Street, the medieval suburb outside the city's control, also developed a flourishing innkeeping trade, at least from the sixteenth century.

From what has been said so far it must be clear that a medieval visitor to Salisbury was given plenty of opportunities to part with his money, whether he was a rich merchant, a local farmer, or a humble pilgrim. Much of the accrued wealth of the city bolstered its tradesmen, who formed themselves into guilds and began to wield increasing power as the peak of prosperity was reached in the fifteenth century. Their struggle for emancipation will be one of the themes of the next chapter. But a proportion of the city's income was garnered by its progenitor and landlord, the bishop of Salisbury. To

The former George Inn, a prestigious High Street property acquired by the city council in 1404

administer the city and to oversee its market
the bishop employed a bailiff, and by 1314 a
bishop's guildhall had been built on the eastern
side of the market place. It survived until 1788
when the present guildhall was erected on the
site. Into the bishop's guildhall came revenue
derived not only from the market tolls, but also

from fines levied on traders who breached the
market rules, from rents on city properties, and
from taxes (known as tallages) imposed on the
citizens. Beneath the guildhall was a prison, and
a pillory is shown prominently in the centre of
the market place on a map of 1610.

The bishop's guildhall
at the end of its life,
during demolition to
make way for the
present guildhall
between Fish Row and
the market place

We have observed that the vigour of
Salisbury's market was detrimental to the
fortunes of nearby towns, and that it
established for itself a large hinterland of
surrounding countryside which depended on it
for goods and services. The riverside villages of
south Wiltshire which had existed before New
Salisbury were of course affected by their
prodigious neighbour. Some found that their
village streets and country lanes were becoming
part of a new traffic pattern, as the road system
became centred on Salisbury rather than on
Wilton or Old Sarum. Milford (that part of it
which was not swallowed up by the new city)
found itself on the road between Salisbury and
Clarendon, and the medieval bridge built to
carry traffic over the River Bourne has survived.
Fisherton Anger, Salisbury's western neighbour,
migrated and expanded to form a
new suburban settlement along
what is now Fisherton Street.
East Harnham, too, readjusted
itself after Harnham Bridge was
built in 1244, so that it could
benefit from the main-road
traffic. Further afield Coombe
Bissett and Homington seem both

Milford Bridge, on the
city's eastern outskirts,
dates from around
1400

The Rose and Crown, Harnham. East Harnham, south of the Avon crossing, was a village which adapted to its new neighbour by developing along the road to the downs from the bridgehead. This inn would have prepared travellers for the long ascent ahead of them

to have gained. But older river crossings, such as those at Stratford-sub-Castle and Ford, both north of the city, and Britford further south, found themselves neglected as traffic dwindled almost to nothing.

Standing in Salisbury market place on a Saturday morning it is easy to appreciate the importance of the twice-weekly trade to the city throughout its history. The same picture of economic dominance that we have painted could be used to illustrate the history of many successful medieval towns. But the population figures suggest that Salisbury was different. It was not just successful — it was outstandingly successful, when other towns were in recession. And to explain that level of success we need to turn to Salisbury's industrial history, and the manufacture of cloth.

5 THE WEB OF FORTUNE

MEDIEVAL SALISBURY was a city entirely
surrounded by sheep. This was a consequence of
the predominant farming practice, which grazed
sheep flocks extensively on the meagre grass of
the chalk downland, and folded them
intensively on the arable fields to manure and
enrich the soil. Wool was an important and
lucrative by-product, both for the large
landowners, with manors scattered across the
chalklands, and for the peasants who made up
their tenantry. Estate managers on large estates,
such as those of the bishop of Winchester, were
by the thirteenth century concentrating on
improving the breeding stock and maximising
output by moving flocks between manors.
Stanley Abbey in north Wiltshire was in about
1275 selling wool from its manors directly to
Italian merchants.

During the first century of Salisbury's
existence the dominant trade was in raw wool
rather than manufactured cloth. That Salisbury
men and women participated in this trade we
know. In 1275 fifteen of them were brought to
book for trying to evade export restrictions, and
in a single year, 1314/15, one Salisbury
merchant exported the wool or fleeces of more
than 6,000 sheep. His name was Robert of
Knoyle, which places him in the same category
as John de Pultone, that is, as a member of a
successful incoming family — Knoyle was a
wool-producing manor of the bishop of
Winchester some twenty miles west of Salisbury.
His success at Salisbury may be gauged by the
fact that he twice served as the city's mayor.
Although there are no statistics we may be
confident that Salisbury's flourishing market
during the early years included a vigorous trade
in wool, so that the city established itself, at
Wilton's expense, as the clearing-house for much
of the wool produced on Salisbury Plain.

During the later fourteenth century there
was a gradual but significant shift, at national
level, away from the export of raw wool, and
towards the production of woollen cloth. An

Sheep in Harnham
meadows

43

Upholding a long tradition. Unloading sheep in Salisbury market place around 1910, an illustration by Bernard Gotch for Hudson's *A Shepherd's Life*

English textile industry developed, both for export and for the home market. This, we recall, was the period when after more than two centuries of growth, England's population and economy declined dramatically. But the decline was not evenly spread. Many towns suffered, especially if they had derived part of their wealth from wool and small-scale traditional clothmaking; some rural areas, by contrast, witnessed growth. The determining factor was the development of the fulling mill, a device which mechanised one process in the manufacture of cloth, and which relied on ample supplies of running water as its source of power. In southern England Winchester and Bristol were among the losers, whilst settlements along the rivers of the Cotswolds and the Wiltshire— Somerset border prospered. Examples which retain evidence of late-medieval prosperity are Castle Combe on the By Brook near Chippenham, and Mells near Frome.

Harnham Mill in the nineteenth century. The building dates from about 1500, with a cloth factory of about 1810 adjoining. Fulling may have begun on the site before 1300

Salisbury, unlike some other towns, seems to have welcomed the new technology. From its five rivers it could harness plentiful natural power, and already during the thirteenth century there are references to fulling mills nearby at Downton, Stratford sub Castle, Steeple

Langford and West Harnham, the latter perhaps
on the site of the present Harnham Mill. They
had been joined, by the sixteenth century, by
other mills, at Quidhampton, Milford, and the
Town Mills next to Fisherton Bridge in the city
centre.

The manufacture of cloth involves a number
of separate processes, including cleaning,
carding (combing the woollen fibres), spinning,
dyeing, weaving, fulling (felting the woven
cloth by beating it) and finishing (including
raising the nap, shearing and pressing). Unlike
the factory-based textile industry of the
nineteenth century, medieval cloth production
was fragmented, and each of the major processes
was the work of a specific craftsman, usually
working independently, or with very few
employees. Looking down the list of taxpayers
in 1332, which we mentioned at the start of
Chapter 4, one notices Nicholas le Deghere (i.e.
Dyer), Henry le Nappere and Stephen le Sherere.

Medieval cottages
in Guilder Lane.
They typify the
weavers' and other
clothworkers'
dwellings and
workplaces which
must once have
occupied much of
Salisbury's eastern
and northern
chequers.

But in 1332 such occupations were
exceptional, and Salisbury's day as a
clothmaking centre was still to come. By the
1380s and 1390s it was a different story.
Another tax list suggests that in about 1400
very roughly one-third of Salisbury's traders
were either weavers, fullers or dyers, and that
more than one-quarter of households in the city
were involved, in some way, in selling finished
cloth. During the fifteenth century the
proportions were higher. A meeting in 1421
attracted about 400 Salisbury weavers and
fullers, and although many of these were
employees, some of the masters have left us
evidence in their wills that their craft had
brought them considerable wealth. A weaver
died in 1473 owning nearly half a chequer, and
others turn up in the records of Southampton's
export and import trade.

The fullers (always known as tuckers in
Wiltshire) seem to have been engaged in all the
finishing processes as well as fulling, and the

dyers — a rather elusive group in Salisbury's history — found their city's market at the heart of an international trade in imported dyestuffs. If we add to these male-dominated crafts that of spinning, which was practised by very many married women as well as 'spinsters', we arrive at a view of late-medieval Salisbury in which nearly every cottage had its loom and its spinning wheel, and where the river was lined with dyers' sheds, and the open spaces festooned with fullers' tentering racks. It had become an industrial city, but not in the modern sense of factories and large employers; this was the domestic industry of countless small businessmen and women, who struck their bargains with each other around the yarn cross in the open market place.

During its heyday in the fifteenth century Salisbury became one of the most important clothmaking centres in the kingdom, and in this respect it almost entirely overshadowed the rest of Wiltshire. Already by 1394/5 seven out of every eight cloths produced in Wiltshire were attributed to Salisbury (although some of these were no doubt produced in the villages around the city). Its speciality was a mid-price brand of striped cloth known as 'Salisbury ray', which must have looked rather like tweed. It was sold not only throughout England, but large quantities were also exported, through Southampton, to much of the known world. This

The north range of Church House, in Crane Street, has been identified as the house of William Lightfoot, a wealthy Salisbury merchant of the mid-fifteenth century

trade, and Salisbury's cloth industry generally, began a long decline from about 1500, as outlets were closed, fashions changed, and a revitalised trade controlled by capitalist clothiers sprang up in new locations. This time Salisbury reacted badly to innovation, and was entering a period of doldrums, but its textile trade remained considerable, and even managed a quiet revival for a few years at the close of the eighteenth century. By then, of course, it was too late.

Medieval Salisbury had a ready supply of the raw material for clothmaking, and a busy population of craft workers. It also had a flourishing market, as we have seen, and it is here, around the fringes of the market place, that we should look to find the other figure in our equation which will explain the city's prosperity. That figure is the merchant, and we can still find many traces of him in the domestic and religious architecture of the city centre.

Before they could be sold, finished cloth had to be inspected by a government official known as an alnager, and from his records we learn that in 1396/7 the greatest number of cloths presented for inspection by a Salisbury

Facing Fish Row, this fourteenth-century house in Queen Street has been misattributed to John a Port, but probably belonged to another wealthy merchant and grocer, John Cammell

businessman during the year was 304. His name was John Coscoumbe, and another eight individuals each presented between 100 and 142 cloths. Nearly 7,000 cloths were attributed to Salisbury during the year. The successors of men such as Coscoumbe, who when given an occupation were generally described as 'mercer', 'draper' or 'clothman', became the leaders of an influential and wealthy merchant class in Salisbury during the fifteenth century.

The merchants stood at the end of the chain of manufacturing processes, and it was their business acumen which maximised the return from the city's handiwork. At their most entrepreneurial the Salisbury merchants owned and operated their own ships out of Southampton, which took finished cloths to the Mediterranean, the Bordeaux region and the Low Countries. Their ships returned laden with luxury goods such as wine, as well as dyestuffs, spices and other exotic items, which were then carried back for sale in Salisbury market.

The names of several of these merchants are still well known in Salisbury by virtue of surviving buildings associated with them. John Halle and John a Port are remembered for their houses next to the market place (although the latter has been wrongly attributed); William Swayne has achieved immortality on account of his chantry chapel in St Thomas's Church. Others, including William Lightfoot who owned Church House in

The Hall of John Halle, in New Canal, sits uncomfortably between nondescript later buildings, and is used as the foyer of a cinema

47

Crane Street, and the anonymous builder of 3/5 Minster Street (Carter's, jewellers, next to the Poultry Cross), have been forgotten. In their day such merchants were major landholders in the city. William Swayne had about twenty-three premises in 1455, and John Halle about sixteen. Their self-assurance and opulent lifestyle appear to have set the trend for their lesser contemporaries, when Salisbury was at the height of its powers.

Almost from Salisbury's inception the city traders had formed themselves into an association, known as a guild merchant. Such guilds existed in many equivalent medieval towns, and often came to assume some of the functions which we associate with local government. This is why the centre of local administration in many towns is called the guildhall. Salisbury's guild merchant had social, religious and ceremonial functions, and came to be associated with St George, on whose day a procession around the city followed by feasting took place. We shall see shortly how this organisation became the fledgling Salisbury corporation, persistently at loggerheads with and rebelling against the bishop's administration of his city.

But by 1380 we start to find references also to guilds representing the interests of specific crafts. A surviving list of 1440 includes no fewer than thirty-eight occupations drawn up in nineteen separate guilds; their representatives attended a meeting to discuss completing the defensive ditch which had been begun around the northern and eastern limits of the city. Stephen Waryn and John Cathero, for example, were the delegates representing a guild of saddlers, cutlers, pewterers, pin-makers and card-makers (cards were wire combs used in preparing wool for spinning). Leatherworkers

Grotesque carved figures support an upstairs window of the joiners' guildhall in St Ann Street

were represented by four guilds: the shoemakers and curriers; the tanners; the skinners; and the bookbinders, parchment-makers and glovers. The most important crafts — including the weavers, fullers, dyers and tailors — each had their own guild. We may assume that every guild had its own guildhall, and two have survived from later in the guilds' history to the present day. The shoemakers' hall is a seventeenth-century building forming part of the Pheasant Inn in Salt Lane; and the flamboyantly carved joiners' hall, also of seventeenth-century date, stands in St Ann Street.

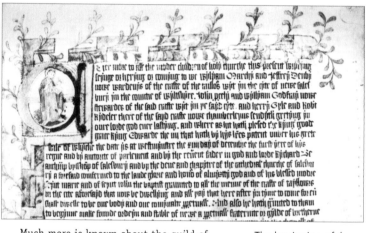

Much more is known about the guild of tailors than about any other. It existed before 1413, and from 1444 onwards an almost complete set of ledgers tell its story. Like any other society part of its business was concerned with membership, including the regulations and codes of practice which members must obey. The members were divided into two fellowships, the masters and the journeymen (employees), and the guild also oversaw apprentices to their craft. A particular concern lay with the spiritual welfare of members. The guild worshipped together, and prayed for the souls of deceased members in the afterlife. Every year at midsummer, on the feast of the birth of their patron saint, St John the Baptist, a day was devoted to solemn prayers and services, a procession and a feast, which included dinner and 'a drynkyng yn the moste godely wyse'. The guild's activities were centred on St Thomas's Church, where they had their own chantry chapel of St John. This was built by William Swayne for the tailors and himself, and is now called the Swayne Chapel. They probably also had their hall in or close to the churchyard, and their procession included a visit to St John's Chapel on Harnham Bridge.

The beginning of the list of ordinances or rules of the tailor's guild, contained in a manuscript book of the fifteenth century

Part of the roof and north wall of the Swayne chapel in St Thomas's church. Wall paintings adorn the chapel and the roof is inscribed with instructions (in Latin) to pray for Swayne and his family

By the end of the middle ages processions and watches included what was referred to as a pageant, and in the sixteenth century we find the first references to the tailors' giant, which must by then have formed the most impressive element in any celebration. Processional giants existed in a number of English cities, but only Salisbury's has survived. He has become associated with another pageant figure, a hobby-horse called Hob-Nob, who perhaps began life as the dragon portrayed during the guild merchant's festival on St George's day. By 1611 the pageant, with its overtones of medieval superstition, was very much out of tune with the prevailing puritan mood, and the tailors were told by the mayor that it was, 'abomynable before god and hell gapes for such ydle and prophane fellowes as delyght in it'. But the giant was preserved, and lived on in the guildhall built by the tailors behind Milford Street in 1534 (which was demolished in 1971/2); in his later years he was paraded around the city on important occasions, such as coronations. In 1873 he was purchased for £1.50 by Salisbury Museum, where he now lives in retirement, alongside his accomplice, Hob-Nob.

Because Salisbury had been founded by the bishop on his own land, and as an adjunct to his cathedral, control of the city's affairs belonged to him. But as its wealth and importance increased, so an elite class of prosperous merchants and businessmen developed, and it was natural that they wished to take a share in, if not complete control over, the government of their city. Their guild merchant, as we have seen, existed from the very early years, and later the craft guilds became important elements in the social and religious life of Salisbury. By 1249 there was a mayor, and the city had been divided into four wards, represented by aldermen. During the fifteenth century, when the city's fortunes were at their highest, there was an elected assembly of two chambers, known as the twenty-four and the forty-eight, which appointed from amongst its members each year the mayor, serjeants, reeves and other officials. In its religious and ceremonial guise this assembly, also known as the mayor and commonalty, was identified with the guild or fraternity of St George, in other words the guild merchant. By 1416 this citizens' body had its own premises, adjoining the Cheesemarket, and between 1573 and 1584 a new Council House was built for it in the centre of the market place, on the site now occupied by the war memorial.

Meanwhile the bishop retained his hold over his city, and we saw in Chapter 4 that he had his own guildhall in the market place to police and control the market. Tension between the citizens and their overlord was inevitable, and first spilled over into rebellion in 1302. Entirely within his rights the bishop imposed a tax on the inhabitants, which they refused to pay. After four years of dispute they capitulated, and agreed with the bishop a humilitaing set of conditions. These permitted the city to appoint its own mayor, on condition that he swore his allegiance to the bishop.

Salisbury's pageant giant, Christopher, with his attendant hobby-horse, Hob-Nob, and various attendants celebrate the coronation in 1911. The giant's black face was the result of varnish applied in the nineteenth century. It was removed, and his Europan complexion restored, during conservation at Salisbury Museum, now his permanent home.

The citizens' Elizabethan council house stood in front of the site of the present guildhall in the market place, where the war memorial is situated. Behind it can be seen the bishop's guildhall. Both buildings were demolished during the 1780s

Smouldering resentment did not erupt into serious confrontation until 1450, but in that year, during Cade's rebellion, the bishop of Salisbury was murdered on Salisbury Plain by a gang which included Salisbury citizens. Such extreme action cannot be directly linked with the struggle for emancipation, but fifteen years later trouble flared again, this time over a dispute between the merchants William Swayne and John Halle. Swayne, with the bishop's permission, had built a house for his chantry priest next to St Thomas's Church. Halle, then mayor, claimed that the plot in question belonged to the citizens' assembly, and pursued their cause with venom and rancour, directed against not only the bishop, but also his old rival Swayne, and ultimately against the king, for which insolence he was imprisoned. The outcome, settled in 1474, spelled humiliation for the citizens once more.

Occasional rebellion by mayors during the sixteenth century culminated from the 1580s onwards in plans to seek incorporation for the city, on the grounds that the two rival administrations were contributing to Salisbury's decline. In 1612 a charter of incorporation was secured from James I, which gave the citizens a large measure of autonomy and reorganized the old medieval guilds into trade companies. To the imaginative generation of puritan administrators who now found themselves in control of Salisbury this independence, so hard-won, must have seemed to be the dawning of a new age of hope and prosperity for their famous city. In the event matters turned out somewhat differently.

6 A BITTERSWEET SOCIETY

THE CITY which in 1612 eagerly celebrated its long-awaited charter of incorporation was a fading regional capital beset with problems. Its days of supremacy as a cloth-making centre were over, besides its own poor it was becoming overburdened with vagrants, every twenty years or so epidemic disease stalked its streets and watercourses, and it was slipping down the league table of the largest English cities – seventh in 1523, fifteenth in 1662. By 1800 it still had its problems; there were slum courtyards lurking down alleyways in the centre of chequers, and the watercourses continued to be a menace to public health. The industrial revolution seemed set to pass it by, and its population was probably slightly lower than it had been three hundred years earlier. And this was against the background of a rapidly rising national population. From a regional capital of international merchants it had become a provincial town of little more than local significance.

But the two centuries separating 1600 from 1800 also saw positive accomplishments. Salisbury achieved excellence in several new or

The Hall, in New Street, built for a clothier as his spacious dwelling house around 1750

revitalized industries, it became the hub of a road network which brought it a lucrative passing trade, its cathedral was becoming a magnet for visitors, and, most important of all, it became 'gentrified'. Rich and respectable members of fashionable society set up home in the Close, in the smarter city chequers, and in the surrounding countryside. They transformed existing houses and built anew, and by patronizing local tradesmen enabled them to prosper and rebuild. It was therefore a time of contrasts, a bittersweet society. And its effect was crucial on the Salisbury which we see today.

During the 1620s the leaders of the new local government in Salisbury, a group of puritan radicals whose power-base was St Edmund's Church and parish, attempted to alleviate poverty in the declining city by introducing a series of innovatory schemes. They reorganised the city workhouse as a kind of retraining centre for the unemployed poor, arranged apprenticeships for pauper children, opened a municipal brewery as a means of generating income for poor relief, and organised a storehouse to supply basic provisions at cost price by a token system of payment. Their idealism, which they said was intended to bring, 'glory to God and profit to the city', was not sufficient to overcome opposition from the richer parish of St Thomas's, nor from the vested interest of the city brewers. By 1642 all the schemes were in abeyance, and a new workhouse, run along conventional lines, had

The courtyard of Trinity Hospital

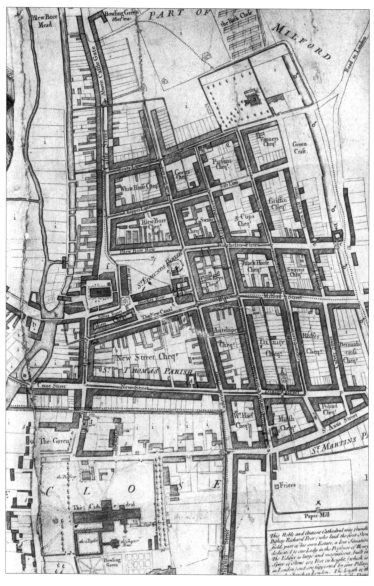

been opened in 1638 in the building now known as Church House in Crane Street.

Another way of tackling the continuing problem of poverty was to endow almshouses. Trinity Hospital, a medieval foundation thought to date from 1379, was brought within the control of the mayor and commonalty by the 1612 charter, and in 1702 it was rebuilt and reorganized. Other surviving almshouses earlier than 1800 were built in 1534 (Brickett's Hospital in Exeter Street, rebuilt in 1780 and 1895), and as a result of gifts or bequests by Margaret Blechynden in 1682 (Greencroft Street), Thomas Taylor in 1695 (Bedwin Street), Edward Frowd in

This finely detailed map of Salisbury by William Naish was first published in 1716, and revised in 1751. It depicts a city rebuilding itself within the confines of its medieval streets, tenements and watercourses

1719 (Bedwin Street), and William Hussey in 1794 (Castle Street). Another, rather special, building of this type stands just within the Close. This is the Matrons' College, founded by Bishop Seth Ward (whom we shall encounter shortly) in 1682 for the widows of clergy in the dioceses of Salisbury and Exeter.

A leading figure in the radicals' approach to poverty, a goldsmith called John Ivie, has achieved local memorability, and even a street within the city chequers named after him. Recorded outbreaks of plague devastated Salisbury in 1563, 1579, 1604, 1627 and 1666. The most severe, in 1604, may have carried off seventeen per cent of the population during a few months. John Ivie was mayor of the city during the next plague year, 1627, and has left a harrowing account of his attempt to maintain law and order, limit the epidemic's severity, and provide for sufferers. He organised a dole of basic foodstuffs, responded with force to any sign of rebellion amongst the watchers and corpse-bearers, and suppressed the alehouses – 'for I will not suffer the city to be undone for to maintain the Devil's school in so many houses'. He tried to stop those tailors who remained in the city from holding their accustomed midsummer feast. Six of them defied his order, held their feast, and five had died of the plague within a week.

Although Salisbury was perhaps no more severely visited by the plague than other cities – indeed in 1625 and 1665 king and court moved to Salisbury to escape the plague in London – two later epidemics, of smallpox in 1723 and cholera in 1849, were correctly attributed to the insanitary state of the watercourses. In 1737 they were realigned and made to flow within brick-lined channels along

After more than two centuries of service to Salisbury and its wide hinterland Salisbury Infirmary closed in 1993, and its functions were transferred to a new district hospital on the city's southern outskirts

the sides of the streets, and between 1851 and 1860, after vigorous campaigning, they were filled in and replaced by conventional water supplies and sewers. The larger and deeper watercourse known as the town ditch survived until 1875, and is still commemorated by the modern name of one of the streets along which it flowed, the New Canal.

The smallpox outbreak of 1723 recurred in 1752, and prompted interest in ways of treating the disease, by inoculation or other means. A smallpox hospital was opened, and in 1766 plans were launched to raise funds for a general hospital or infirmary for the city. Salisbury Infirmary opened to patients in its purpose-built premises in Fisherton Street in 1771. With many later additions this imposing building continued in its medical role until 1993, and has since been converted to houses and apartments.

Fisherton Street lay outside the medieval grid plan of city chequers, and beyond the jurisdiction of the city authorities. It had nevertheless functioned as a suburb of Salisbury since the middle ages, and had attracted urban buildings along it, including a Dominican friary in 1281, and a gaol by 1421. They lay on opposite sides of the street immediately next to Fisherton Bridge against the river, and the present clock tower incorporates eighteenth-century masonry from the gaol. During the seventeenth century the number of inns and alehouses increased along Fisherton Street and in Fisherton generally, so that by 1686 accommodating travellers and their horses had become a speciality of the parish. Salisbury and Fisherton together could at this date accommodate 630 guests and nearly 1,000 horses.

Salisbury, as we have seen, had established its position along a main road very early in its career, through the construction of Harnham Bridge in about 1244. Overland travel increased markedly during the sixteenth and seventeenth centuries, and by 1700 the city found itself at the hub of a road network. From London the route to the south-west divided at Salisbury into a number of strands, including roads via Mere towards north Devon, via Shaftesbury or Blandford to Exeter, and via Cranborne to Poole. In addition there was a main road from Southampton to Bristol, and others running northwards from the city across Salisbury Plain to Oxford and Gloucestershire. Several of these roads, and others, were improved by turnpiking during the eighteenth century, and measures were taken to cleanse and repair the increasingly traffic-laden city streets.

After turnpiking, the road network could carry swifter and more reliable passenger

The Victorian clock tower beside Fisherton Bridge incorporates stone, including a carving of manacles, from the gaol which occupied the site

vehicles. The six stagecoaches which plied between London and Salisbury each week in 1763 had increased to fifty-two in 1795. During the peak year of coaching, 1839, over 50,000 passengers were carried by public and private coaches on this route alone. By this date there were fifty-nine scheduled coaches weekly to London, forty to Southampton and thirty-one to Bath, as well as routes to Exeter, Devizes and towns along the south coast.

The former Black Horse inn, one of Salisbury's leading coaching inns, went out of business after the coaching traffic dwindled away after 1840

The city's importance as a staging-point for coaches and stopping-place for travellers may have given the highway surveyors a headache, but it was very good news for the innkeepers. As in Fisherton Street so in the city chequers the number of inns increased during the seventeenth and eighteenth centuries, many of them incorporating portions of medieval houses. A map of the city first published in 1716 records the name then used to describe each chequer, and most are named after prominent inns, such as Three Swans, Three Cups, White Horse, Cross Keys and Antelope. Two such chequers, White Hart and Black Horse, commemorate inns which

The White Hart, its principal rival for the coaching trade, has survived and flourished

were to become the principal coaching establishments of the city. The Black Horse, on the corner of Winchester Street and Brown Street, is no longer an inn; but the present White Hart, with its handsome classical facade of about 1820, and slightly later upstairs assembly room, is a good demonstration of the money which travelled with the stagecoach passenger.

The travelling public offered some of Salisbury's craftsmen an additional market for their wares. Cutlers, for example, were represented in the list of guilds drawn up in 1440, and many medieval knives have survived in Salisbury Museum's drainage collection. Recent excavations on medieval sites in the city have found evidence of hornworking, an industry which may have included the production of handles for knives. After the 1612 charter cutlers were grouped with armourers, and some Salisbury cutlers seem to have specialized in making edged weapons. But during the seventeenth century their reputation was made on high quality razors, scissors and knives. Guidebooks of the coaching period refer to cutlery as a Salisbury speciality, and selections of wares were put on display and sold to passing stagecoach passengers.

Cutlery is an example of an old town craft which enjoyed a renaissance in Salisbury. Another was joinery, which included the making not only of furniture, but also of architectural woodwork. Solid Jacobean oak furniture, with finely carved figures and decoration, emanated from the workshops of the Salisbury joiners, and enjoyed a vogue in south Wiltshire and beyond. Examples still to be seen in Salisbury include a mayoral chair in Salisbury Museum, the tomb panel to Humphrey Beckham ('his own worke') in St Thomas's Church, and the carved facade of the joiners' own guildhall in St Ann Street.

Here underlyeth the Body
of HumphreyBeckham
who died the 2ⁿᵈ day
of February Anno 1671
Aged 83 Yᵣˢ.
His own Worke

Monument in St Thomas's Church to Humphry Beckham, doyen of Salisbury joiners, and 'his own worke'

Two other Salisbury manufactures of the period, without medieval antecedents, were bonelace and clay pipes. A petition of about 1700 claimed that there were then over one thousand lace-makers in Salisbury, or more than one in seven of the population, and that a single lace dealer was sending lace worth between £60 and £80 to London each week. The lace-makers would have been largely poor women and children, but the 'lacemen' or dealers could be men of influence, and included at least one mayor of Salisbury, Richard Minifie in 1681. Pipemakers existed in most towns, and flourished during the eighteenth century when tobacco was cheap and fashionable. Because they stamped their name or mark on their products it is sometimes possible to link documentary and archaeological evidence of

Malmesbury House in the Close, the home of James Harris and his family. His music room adjoined the house, above St Ann's Gate, to the right of the picture

their activities. An archaeological excavation conducted in 1987/8 in Brown Street, close to Trinity Hospital, uncovered pipes and pipemaking debris from the workshop of a certain Joel Sanger. His working life seems to have extended from about 1710 to 1740, and he died in 1750. His will mentions the workshops and other buildings which he owned in Brown Street. He seems to have been a second or even third generation pipemaker, but his sons adopted other trades; by 1750 the pipemaking industry was in decline.

If Joel Sanger, the industrious tradesman, represents one stratum of eighteenth-century Salisbury society, some two hundred yards away from his back-street workshop could have been found the representative of another. James Harris lived in an elegant mansion (now called Malmesbury House) which his father had built in 1705 next to St Ann's Gate. In the year after Sanger's death Harris published an acclaimed study of ancient philosophy which he called *Hermes*; thereafter he was nicknamed 'Hermes' Harris. 'Hermes' distinguished himself not only in literary and dramatic circles (he was a close friend of Henry Fielding, and knew Samuel Richardson, Fanny Burney, David Garrick and Dr Johnson); in his later years he served in Parliament, rising to hold posts in the Admiralty and the Treasury, before becoming secretary and comptroller of the queen's household. He has been described as Wiltshire's *arbiter elegantiarum*, or 'judge of taste', a kind of 'Beau Nash' for Salisbury.

The comparison with Bath is not too far-fetched. Since the episcopate of Seth Ward (1667-89), who was a respected scientist and a founding member of the Royal Society, Salisbury had been developing as a place of learning, culture and high society. Ward, like Harris, had a circle of eminent friends, and these included Sir Christopher Wren (whom he called in to advise on the state of the cathedral fabric), the mathematician Sir Isaac Newton, the

philosopher Thomas Hobbes, the diarist Samuel
Pepys, and no less a figure than the king,
Charles II, himself. Wren and Hobbes were
natives of the diocese, and several lesser figures
in the scientific world were attracted by Ward's
presence at Salisbury to take up residence in the
city themselves.

Under James Harris eighteenth-century
Salisbury maintained its reputation as a place of
culture and refinement. A contemporary of
Harris, Benjamin Collins, began a successful and
profitable business as bookseller and publisher
in the city, and developed one of the earliest
and most influential provincial newspapers, the
Salisbury & Winchester Journal, which has been
published continuously since 1729. Another
contemporary, Benjamin Banks, produced from
his workshop in Catherine Street some of the
finest violins ever made in England. And Harris
himself initiated a vigorous musical life in the
city, by organizing an annual Salisbury Music
Festival at which he championed the music of
his friend, the composer Handel – some of
whose works were published by Collins. The
diaries of both Harris and a later composer,
John Marsh, have recently been published,
and offer vivid descriptions of high society in
the Salisbury of their day.

Such Olympian associations, which could
easily be supplemented by others, were
naturally of great importance to Salisbury's
status and reputation at the time. But they
have also had more lasting and tangible
effects. One consequence of the reformation,
more than a century before Ward's arrival, had
been to release as private residences for
laymen houses in the Close which had
previously been required for cathedral
officials. Rough treatment during the civil war
and commonwealth period in the mid-
seventeenth century had further secularized
the Close, so that after the restoration there was
scope for tasteful and sumptuous redevelopment
on the sites of the old canons' houses. Part of
what is now Sarum College and several of the

The entrance to
Mompesson House,
perhaps the finest
house in the Close,
seen through its
original railings of
1701

Sarum College was
built about 1677 as a
private dwelling house,
by a prominent
Salisbury lawyer,
Francis Hill. It typifies
the gentrification of the
Close at this period

smaller houses date from the 1660s and 1670s, and the Matrons' College was built in 1682. But the grandest houses are a generation later. Thomas Mompesson's textbook house of 1701 overlooking Chorister's Green was followed in 1705, as we have seen, by the Harris family home, Malmesbury House, and then a few years later by several distinguished pieces of work, including Arundells, the Walton Canonry, and Myles Place.

Bourne Hill, next to St Edmund's Church, the grandest town house in Salisbury outside the Close

Investment by the gentry in Salisbury houses was not restricted to the Close. The grandest house in the city was built on the site of the collegiate buildings attached to the medieval St Edmund's Church, and was known as the College until taken over as offices for the local authority in 1927. It is now known as the Council House, or Bourne Hill. Parts of it date from the sixteenth century, but most is the result of successive improvements by the Wyndham family, its owners from 1660. Another distinguished town house, built in the mid-eighteenth century for a successful clothier (and a reminder that the city's textile industry was still by no means dead), is in New Street. Known as the Hall, and now used as solicitors' offices, its street frontage is symmetrical, flanking a porch which projects across the pavement. The best street of eighteenth-century domestic architecture is St Ann Street, but there are also good individual houses in Castle Street and elsewhere.

Many of the smart houses of restoration and Georgian Salisbury have served a spell as private schools. Such schools, to be distinguished from the city grammar school, founded in 1569, and various charity schools operating for the poor and deserving, burgeoned in the polite climate of Salisbury during the century after 1750. Mrs Voysey's school, for example, occupied part of the King's House in the Close (now Salisbury Museum) between 1786 and 1799, and advertised that it catered, 'for the reception of

young ladies, who will be genteely boarded and carefully taught...'. Another school in the Close, with a much longer history, existed to educate the cathedral choristers. From 1714 until 1947 it occupied the purpose-built Queen Anne brick house which is now known as Wren Hall. The school has given its name to the adjacent Choristers' Green.

Two decisions taken by the city intelligentsia during the 1780s sum up the spirit of the age. A fire which damaged the Elizabethan council house in the market place in 1780 offered the pretext to remove a quaint, if rather uncouth, public building, and at the same time to demolish the bishop's medieval guildhall. In their place rose between 1787 and 1795 the present classical guildhall, the gift to the city of a local nobleman, the Earl of Radnor.

Parallel with this development in the city centre was another in the Close. Bishop Shute Barrington, who arrived in 1782, rich and sophisticated, was an admirer of the cathedral.

Wren Hall (right), formerly the chorister's school, with Braybrooke (left), the schoolmaster's house

Salisbury Guildhall, in the market square, replaced the separate administrative buildings of the bishop and his citizens after a fire in 1780

James Wyatt removed the high altar from the chancel so as to give an uninterrupted vista along the eastern half of the cathedral. This view westward from the Trinity Chapel across the ambulatory or retrochoir to the chancel depicts figures walking where the altar had been

But certain features, such as the chantry chapels, the memorials and various other medieval and later accretions, displeased him. He also disliked the medieval glass in the windows and the wall paintings, which interfered with the purity and clarity of the architecture. The dilapidated bell tower in the Close and the graveyard littered with tombstones offended him. Between 1788 and 1791 he employed the architect James Wyatt to correct all these shortcomings, thus sweeping clean from the cathedral and its surroundings much of historical interest and medieval beauty, whilst imposing on a thirteenth-century building eighteenth-century ideals of good taste and design. Much criticized at the time and subsequently, the most irreverential criticism was perhaps that of William Beckford, who described the transformed cathedral as looking like a 'scantily-clad whore'.

7 IN NO WAY DIMINISHED?

'"SHALL WE GO and sit in the Cathedral?" he asked, when their meal was finished.

'"Cathedral? Yes. Though I think I'd rather sit in the railway station," she answered, a remnant of vexation still in her voice. "That's the centre of the town life now. The Cathedral has had its day!"

'"How modern you are!"'

The views expressed by Thomas Hardy's fictional lovers, Jude and Sue, over their meal in a Salisbury inn were perhaps those also of their creator. Two of his poems, *The Impercipient* and *A Cathedral Facade at Midnight* seem to voice his sadness at what seemed to him the irrelevance and implausibility of everything which the cathedral represented. A similar attitude was noticed by the naturalist W.H. Hudson. Writing about the cathedral a few years after Hardy, in 1910, he remarked that the south Wiltshire villager was extremely familiar with it, from a distance. 'But he is not familiar with the interior of the great fane; it fails to draw him, doubtless because he has no time in his busy, practical life for the cultivation of the aesthetic faculties. There is a crust over that part of his mind.'

This kind of question, and especially the attitude of the city to itself and its cathedral, seems to lie at the heart of Salisbury's history over the last two centuries. Was the city trying to regain its medieval position as the regional capital of the area which Hardy dubbed 'Wessex' – and so to become an industrial and commercial metropolis which by now, Bristol fashion, would have had tower blocks overshadowing its historic centre and cathedral? Or was it content to luxuriate in its architecture and history, and await the tourist coaches?

With its new guildhall, its prosperous stagecoach trade and its elegant society Salisbury in 1800 could perhaps be looking forward to a bright future. There was a nagging awareness among its businessmen that it was being overtaken by the new industrial towns of the midlands and north, and this is best seen in their attempt to build a canal which would link Salisbury to Southampton. The project, talked about since 1792, begun in 1795, bankrupt by 1799, and abandoned after 1808, was hardly a success.

Nevertheless the city began to grow. Its population of 7,600 in 1800 had reached 10,000 by 1840, which was higher than ever before; but it was still slightly below the average growth for Wiltshire, and much less than for England and Wales generally. Even so, the first signs of suburban expansion, villas at Harnham and along the Wilton Road, were making their appearance.

A further reason for optimism in 1800, but disappointment soon after, was the state of Salisbury's textile industry. New products, such as flannel, striped cloth and linsey-woolsey, as well as the introduction of machinery, had led to a resurgence of the old mainstay after 1780. The king himself ordered Salisbury cloth, and precipitated a heavy demand. A clothier was mayor in 1784, and twenty-four Salisbury cloth-iers were listed in a directory in 1798. But by 1820 the boom was over, the export market, especially to Portugal, had collapsed, and severe competition from Lancashire cotton was damaging the trade at home. In Salisbury the industry dwindled, and by 1840 had gone altogether.

The next setback was the city's tardiness in jumping on the railway bandwagon. Salisbury, in common with the rest of Wessex, missed out on the first wave of railway building, which between 1839 and 1844 linked most of England's major cities to London and each other. Then during the railway mania of 1844-7 the city backed the wrong horse, a grandiose but dubious scheme called the Manchester and Southampton Railway, which came to nothing. Eventually in 1847, nearly a decade after some potential rivals, a branch line from Southampton was opened. It was to be another dozen years before Salisbury took its place as an important railway junction.

Suburban develop-ment along the Wilton Road, Fisherton

Brunel's railway terminus for the line from Bath and Warminster, opened in 1856, survives but is no longer in railway use

Salisbury railway station buildings of 1902 (left) and 1859 (right)

Was all this a sign that the city was not really trying to promote itself? Probably not. The hope expressed when the first railway arrived was that Salisbury would become the Manchester of the south – probably an envious reference to Lancashire's textile industry, but perhaps also a swipe at the discredited Manchester and Southampton railway company. Two further indications that mid-century Salisbury was trying to advance its position may be seen in the staging of 'the Salisbury Exhibition of Local Industry, Art, Antiquities, Etc.' in the guildhall in 1852, and the erection of a grand covered market house with its own railway connection in 1859.

The former was of course a local imitation of the Great Exhibition at Crystal Palace in 1851, which had given many ordinary people their first real taste of the outside world. It was the first of many staged in provincial towns with the aim of trumpeting local skills and products. The latter was recognition that railways were

The scene inside the guildhall during the Salisbury Exhibition of 1852

The market house façade of 1859 still dominates one side of the market place, although its hall and branch railway have gone, replaced by the public library

altering the whole pattern of marketing, that small town markets were losing their importance as travel became easier, and that the larger, well-connected market towns stood to gain. The aim of making Salisbury market more attractive to farmers and dealers was an immediate and lasting success. W.H. Hudson, seeing the market house in action some fifty years later, described it as, 'like a huge beehive, humming with the noise of talk, full of brown-faced farmers'. It continued in use until 1965, and its classical façade continues to oversee the market place, although now it graces the public library.

Salisbury's attempt to become a manufacturing and industrial town continued. Around the station in Fisherton developed a large working-class suburb during the 1860s and 1870s, and many of its inhabitants found employment on the railways. An important leather-currying business developed and expanded its Endless Street factory, to become by 1897 (so it claimed) the largest concern of its kind in the west of England, with over one hundred employees. A few years later a clock-making business diversified to pioneer the manufacture of motor-cars in Wiltshire, and, as Scout Motors, moved into new premises at Churchfields, Fisherton in 1907. Its rapid success up to 1914 portended a future for Salisbury not so much as another Manchester, but rather as another Coventry. However, the war, and the slump of 1921-2 killed off this possibility, and no other industry has arrived to dominate Salisbury's economic life during the twentieth century in the way that textiles dominated the medieval city.

What then of the other two legs of the three-legged stool upon which (as we suggested in chapter five) Salisbury's prosperity depended? Its role as a market, now in the guise of a shopping, service and administrative centre for south Wiltshire and beyond, has continued to flourish. This, more than anything, has boosted the city's population since 1840 roughly in line with the national trend, from about 13,000 in 1870, to 17,000 in 1900, and around 40,000 (depending where you draw the line) today. Such an increase, coupled with the demolition of sub-standard cottages in the city centre, has led to a predictable suburbanization. This has been most marked along the main routes leading north, north-west and west, although Harnham and Laverstock too, south and east of the city, have taken their share. Fisherton, moreover, has entirely lost its identity as a village independent of the upstart city.

Although in most respects Salisbury's growth since 1840 has been typical of hundreds of other provincial English towns – with their housing and industrial estates, and their infrastructures of schools and community buildings, roads and shops – nevertheless there have been two special factors at work to shape Salisbury's development. First has been the presence, in and around the city, of three large and important institutions. Two were private lunatic asylums, at Fisherton House and Laverstock House, and they pioneered the advancement of psychiatric medicine during the nineteenth century. Fisherton House, later known as Old Manor Hospital, became the largest licensed asylum in England, and between 1850 and 1872 it specialized in the treatment of criminal lunatics. The third institution was very

A building of the former Fisherton House asylum, later the Old Manor Hospital, awaiting renovation in 2004

69

different; it was the diocesan training college for schoolmistresses, which was established in 1841. From 1851 until its demise (as the College of Sarum St Michael) in 1978 it had its home at the King's House in the Close, once Mrs Voysey's academy, and now continuing its educational role as Salisbury and South Wiltshire Museum.

Physical education on the lawn behind the King's House (now Salisbury & South Wiltshire Museum), when it was the diocesan training college

The other special factor in Salisbury's progress as a local centre has been the presence nearby of important military establishments. Although the city itself is not a garrison town, the permanent use since 1897 of much of Salisbury Plain for military training has led to the creation of camps and barracks at Tidworth, Bulford, Larkhill and elsewhere. These, as well as experimental establishments at Boscombe Down and Porton Down, and administrative headquarters at Wilton, are all within easy reach of Salisbury, and their large transient populations are dependent upon the city for shops, services and entertainments. This has had a particular impact on the city during the two world wars of the twentieth century.

And so we return to the last leg of the metaphorical stool, Salisbury Cathedral. Already distanced from the bishop by the charter of incorporation in 1612, the city was further estranged in 1785 when the bishop agreed to the demolition of his guildhall in the market place, the last tangible evidence of his authority. Municipal reform in 1836 made the divorce complete. More than most cathedral cities there exists at Salisbury a clear demarcation between its two components. As Hudson noted in 1910, many people visit Salisbury regularly to shop and do business, without ever venturing into the Close. This is still true. And many visitors from around the world each year make their pilgrimage to the cathedral without ever venturing into the world of the city.

Nevertheless, tourism has become a major ingredient in Salisbury's economy. In this respect the city has always benefited from the proximity of Stonehenge, a mere ten miles away to the north. The earliest surviving account of an excursion made from Salisbury to Stonehenge dates from 1562, and by the eighteenth century intellectuals thought it clever to view Stonehenge and the cathedral on the same day, so as to compare rudeness and perfection in architecture. The first history of Salisbury Cathedral, published in 1723, coupled it with Bath Abbey, and the first guidebook appeared in 1753. It was entitled *A series of particular and useful Observations made with great diligence and care, upon that admirable Structure the Cathedral Church of Salisbury*. It ran to several editions, and was not replaced until 1792, by which date Wyatt's alterations had rendered it obsolete.

Tourism for the masses was, of course, stimulated to a very great extent by the arrival of the railway, and later by the various means of personal mobility. On my bookshelves is an 1884 guide to England and Wales, 'particularly adapted to the use of bicyclists and tricyclists'; it praises especially the elegance of Salisbury Cathedral and the richness of its sepulchral monuments (although it says nothing about the city).

During the twentieth century the number of visitors increased dramatically. A writer in 1977, Dorothy Bradshaw, recalling the Salisbury of her childhood, made the following observations: 'Fifty years ago, only a few clergy went decorously about their business in the Close, and a few sightseers wandered awed and quiet. Now the perimeter of the Close itself has become a large coach and car park, and tourists of every nationality and age stroll, chatter, and picnic within it. But the cathedral is in no way diminished.'

This brings us back to our original question, about the city's aims and attitudes towards itself and its cathedral. The history of the last two centuries suggests that Salisbury did indeed wish to become a major manufacturing city, such as Bristol or Manchester or Coventry. It failed to achieve this aim, but new life was breathed into its marketing and servicing role, partly through its own efforts, but also by the arrival of new neighbours, the armed forces on Salisbury Plain. And because in consequence its growth has been modest, it has not destroyed the character and beauty which residents and visitors so much appreciate. The city may be different from that of Richard Poore or William Swayne, John Ivie or Thomas Hardy, but its essence is in no way diminished.

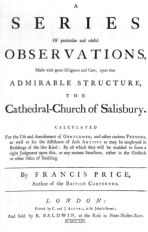

The first Salisbury Cathedral guidebook, published in 1753

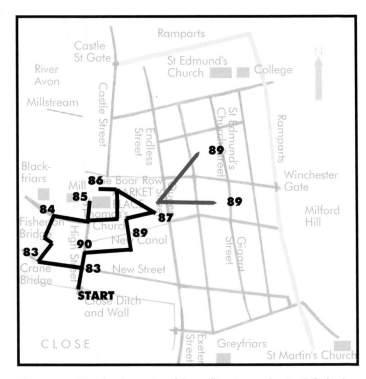

These maps describe the routes of the walking tours, chapter 8 (below), and chapter 9 (above). The numbers refer to the page on which you will find the relevant instructions.

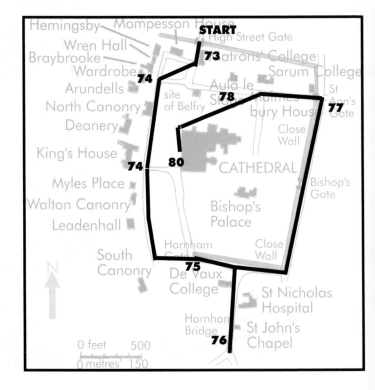

8 A WALK AROUND THE CLOSE

This walk begins at the High Street Gate and proceeds right through the Close and out at Harnham Gate. After visiting Harnham Bridge it returns alongside the Close wall and re-enters the Close by St Ann's Gate. It concludes with a brief exploration of the cathedral interior. If time and energy are limited the tour may be shortened by omitting Harnham Bridge, as indicated in the text. Please bear in mind that, with few exceptions, the houses of the close are private dwellings. Refreshments are normally available at Salisbury and South Wiltshire Museum, Redcoats in the Wardrobe, Mompesson House, the Medieval Hall and Salisbury Cathedral.

High Street Gate, also referred to as the North Gate, is more than a piece of late-medieval architecture. It is a tangible reminder that in Salisbury, more than in most cathedral cities, the town and the Close are two different worlds, and the gate is still shut between them every night. The boundary demarcated by the gate is an original feature of the town plan, but the gate itself, of fourteenth- and fifteenth-century date, forms part of the scheme begun in 1331 to build a wall around the Close. The niche above the arch, seen from the Close side, now contains a statue of Edward VII, but Henry III was probably its first occupant.

Walk through the gate towards the cathedral, concentrating on the buildings on your left.

After the Porter's Lodge (no.48), which retains fourteenth-century details, comes the Matrons' College. This dates from 1682, and was founded as an almshouse for the widows of priests ordained in Salisbury or Exeter dioceses. The bishop who established it, Seth Ward, was an enlightened man who moved in the leading scientific and artistic circles of his day. Something of the influence of his friend, Christopher Wren, may have rubbed off on the design of this symmetrical brick building, with octagonal lantern over the centre and wings projecting at each end. The royal arms and a Latin inscription recording Ward's generosity surmount the entrance. The matrons' windows look across the narrow street at houses which include the dwelling of the Close constable.

73

The street opens out and there is a grassed rectangular area. Walk across or around this until you are at the corner furthest from the Matron's College.

This is Choristers' Green, so-called because one of the eighteenth-century houses on its western side, Wren Hall (no.56), was built for the Choristers' School in 1714 and occupied by them until 1947. The most imposing house overlooking the green is Mompesson House, which stands on the northern side. It belongs to the National Trust and is open to the public during the summer months. It is one of the best examples of the way in which the Close attracted wealthy and respectable laymen during the decades after the restoration in 1660. It was built for the Mompesson family and completed in 1701. With its symmetrical facade of seven stone-built bays, beneath a hipped roof and behind elaborate wrought-iron gates it is often regarded as the perfect example of the Wren-style house.

The eighteenth-century process of replacing or rebuilding medieval houses is well seen around the north-western corner of the green. Next to Mompesson House the Hungerford Chantry is a rebuild of a medieval chantry, and then turning the corner the first house (no.56a-b) is late medieval with fourteenth-century fragments, and extensively rebuilt in 1727. It originated as the residence of the first warden of the Choristers' School, Alexander of Hemingsby, and is named after him. Next to it is Wren Hall, and then Braybrooke House (no.57), the schoolmaster's dwelling.

From Choristers' Green you should now walk southwards along the West Walk of the Close.

The plots laid out and allotted for the canons' houses along the West Walk probably soon after 1200 extend back to the River Avon. A great variety of architectural styles and periods is now to be seen in the houses which occupy these plots. First is an extraordinary building called the Wardrobe, because its site was occupied by the bishop's storehouse; it was refurbished in 2002 and is open to the public as 'Redcoats in the Wardrobe', a military museum for the local regiment. Next comes a coy eighteenth-century house (Arundells) set back behind massive gates, and then, breasting the street, is the North Canonry, mostly sixteenth-century and later.

Next come buildings made or adapted for the use of the diocesan training college for schoomistresses, which occupied the complex between 1851 and 1978. Hidden behind them is an important medieval survivor, the Old Deanery (now called the Medieval Hall), which is usually open to the public with historic displays. Many of the college buildings are now residential apartments, but their centrepiece, the building known as the King's House, has since 1981 housed Salisbury and South Wiltshire Museum.

It originated as the prebendal house of the abbots of Sherborne, and was rebuilt during the fifteenth century. Much of this work survives, as well as the slightly later entrance porch, and a brick cross-wing of about 1600 added after the building had become a private house. Further alterations and adaptations have been made since 1800. A visit to the museum, with its splendid modern galleries devoted to the local history, archaeology and cultural life of the city and its region, is essential for anyone interested in the subject matter of this book.

The King's House looks across to the west front of the cathedral. To do this justice the observer should blank out with their hand in front of their face the spire and the upper stages of the tower, thus restoring the cathedral to its form when the west front was conceived and built. West fronts were architectural showpieces, taken to their extremes in England at Peterborough and Lincoln. But Salisbury's exemplar was Wells, which was built in about 1230, some thirty years before Salisbury. The statuary accommodated in its niches, a theological scheme – never completed – of prophets, saints and Biblical figures, was largely absent or was crumbling away by the time of the Victorian restoration in 1860-75, and most of the present figures date from this period. To the right of the west front notice the low blank wall with its parapet of arcading. This is the west wall of the cloister, and reminds us that Salisbury was a secular cathedral, whose staff were not monks living in buildings attached to a cloister, but canons with individual houses in the Close. Salisbury's cloister, therefore, was added as a processional walkway, and did not form the centrepiece of monastic buildings.

From the King's House continue southward along the West Walk, turning east at the far end past the car park until you reach Harnham Gate at the very southern end of the Close. (If you wish to shorten the walk make your way instead from the King's House up to the west front of the cathedral, and then diagonally across to the North Walk of the Close. Turn to page 78 below to resume the description.)

The southward continuation of the West Walk is a secluded part of the Close, and it contains three excellent examples of eighteenth-century gentrification. They are neighbours (nos.68-70), and in their present form all date from about 1720. Myles Place to the north and Leadenhall to the south flank the Walton Canonry,

so-called because it was once the home of the famous angler's son, Canon Isaac Walton. Leadenhall is on the site of Elias of Dereham's prototype canon's house, begun in 1221 and finally demolished in 1915. At the southern end of the West Walk is the driveway to a large and secluded house, the South Canonry, now a predominantly late-Victorian building, and the residence of the bishop. The home of his predecessors until 1946, the Bishop's Palace, is also hidden from view. As we turn to admire the excellent view of the cathedral, it lies beyond the trees and wall running south from the cloister. Altered and improved by many bishops, it still retains traces of its thirteenth-century origin. It is now the Cathedral School. Harnham Gate, our exit from the Close, is contemporary with the Close Wall, and so was built in the mid-fourteenth century.

Walk out through Harnham Gate, and along the narrow road (De Vaux Place) as far as the corner. Then turn right and, noting buildings on both sides, make your way to the bridge.

A well-preserved section of the Close Wall accompanies our walk along De Vaux Place. The building on the corner, De Vaux House, sports a rough flint wall with a chimneybreast and a small buttress. This is a fragment of the fledgling medieval university of Salisbury, known as De Vaux College, or 'the house of the valley of scholars'. The name derives from a similar French attempt to found an 'alternative' university, and attracted Oxford students during the thirteenth century and later. The present De Vaux House displays the arms of Oxford University in recognition of this link.

Further along the road to the bridge (St Nicholas's Road), on the left, is another thirteenth-century establishment, the Hospital of St Nicholas. Parts of the fabric of the two ranges, facing each other north and south across a courtyard, date from the first few years of the new city's existence. The arcade which once ran along the centre of a larger, aisled, south range is now incorporated in its outside wall. The whole complex underwent very obvious and extensive restoration by the Victorians. As a charitable institution it survived the reform-

ation, and has continued to the present to function as an almshouse. In 1851 a visitor to Salisbury exploring in this area found inspir-ation from the venerable building for the first of a famous series of novels. His name was Anthony Trollope, and Hiram's Hospital in *The Warden*, the first of the Barsetshire series, was conceived here, although its later elaboration owed much more to Winchester and Wells than to Salisbury.

And so we reach the bridge, or rather the two bridges, since they are divided by a small island in the river. On this island the unprepossessing rendered house to the left of the road is actually a thirteenth-century chapel for travellers using the bridge. It was dedicated to St John, fell out of use at the reformation, and was converted to a house in about 1800. A medieval doorway and window may still be seen from the road. Harnham Bridge crosses the River Avon, here augmented by the River Nadder, close to the site of an earlier ford, and like the chapel was built by Bishop Bingham in about 1244. It was a crucial factor in the success of the new city, since it diverted main road traffic to the west country away from Salisbury's rival, Wilton, and directed travellers through the city streets. The two sections of the bridge were widened in 1774, and continued to carry all main road traffic south from the city until 1933.

Before retracing our steps it is worthwhile crossing the bridge and continuing for a few paces, not only to catch sight of the striking timber-framing displayed in the curved frontage of the fourteenth-century north range of the Rose and Crown Hotel, but also, looking back, to enjoy a glimpse of the cathedral spire as it forms a backcloth to the view of the bridge.

Return along St Nicholas's Road (on the left-hand pavement) to the corner by De Vaux House, cross De Vaux Place and turn right, so that you are walking next to the battlemented Close Wall. This will bring you shortly to a heavily-trafficked roundabout. Follow the wall around to the left, and walk the length of Exeter Street, back towards the city. After rather more than 400 yards you will find yourself at St Ann's Gate, opposite the beginning of St Ann Street.

Exeter Street is part of an early street alignment, referred to as 'high street' in early documents, which was integral to the plan of New Salisbury. It carried (and still carries) traffic from the south into the city, and demarcated the eastern limit of the Close. The wall, which since the fourteenth century has formed an effective barrier between the street and the Close, was built with reused stone from the Norman cathedral at Old Sarum. Mason's marks, carved roundel decorations and other fragments of sculpture from the old cathedral have been incorporated into the wall, and may be seen in many places, especially near the far end, opposite the building known as Cathedral Court. There is a medieval gate along this stretch of wall, which was built to give access to the Bishop's Palace.

Ribbon development had occurred along Exeter Street opposite the wall by the sixteenth century, and several cottages of this period have survived, although with later façades. Note also

a range of almshouses, Bricketts Hospital, which was founded in 1534 but rebuilt in 1895, and the Catholic church dedicated to St Osmund. This was built, largely of flint, in 1847-8 to the designs of Augustus Pugin, who had spent several years as a young man in the nearby village of Alderbury.

St Ann's Gate, which leads us back into the Close, is contemporary with the building of the wall; the room above it was used during the eighteenth century for concerts, which included early performances of the music of Handel. The composer himself is believed to have performed there on at least one occasion.

Enter the Close by St Ann's Gate and make your way along the North Walk until it is joined by the Bishop's Walk on the left, where the cathedral graveyard wall begins. Take the diagonal path back to the front of the cathedral. (If you decided to shorten your walk when you reached the King's House you should pick up the description again at this point.)

Next to St Ann's Gate is one of the most lavish of the eighteenth-century additions to the architecture of the Close. Malmesbury House was the home of James 'Hermes' Harris, who made an appearance in chapter six as the leader of Georgian Salisbury's culture and society. The house, sometimes open to the public, has a sumptuous interior, fine gardens, and a memorable painted sundial (of 1749), which is visible from the north walk.

The domestic architecture of this part of the Close is in general more modest than around Choristers' Green or along the West Walk; indeed there is a lane of cottages (Rosemary Lane) running north to the Close wall. But two buildings are of greater interest. The centrepiece of Sarum College (which was established in 1860 as the diocesan theological college) is a large house of about 1677, and therefore a generation earlier than most of the gentry houses in the Close. Nearby, the building known as 'Aula le Stage' (no.21) is one of the best-preserved of the medieval canon's houses, with surviving thirteenth-century architecture behind a double-gabled Elizabethan front of flint. Near the corner of Choristers' Green it will be noticed that there are several small houses apparently built within the cathedral graveyard, on the southern side of the North Walk. These mark the approximate position of the detached bell tower or campanile, around which they had been built. The tower, which was contemporary with the building of the cathedral, was demolished in 1790.

Now it is time to turn our attention to the exterior of the cathedral itself. We have already examined the west front, and now, from this new vantage point along the diagonal path north of the nave, we should again mask out the spire and upper stages of the tower from our vision, in order to recover the appearance of the original building.

Salisbury differs from all other medieval English cathedrals in the unity of its composition. Work began at the east end in 1220, and proceeded westwards for nearly five decades until the west front was completed. The style which we call Early English had been familiar in England for no more than forty years when Salisbury was begun, and although minor alterations were introduced as the work progressed, no major changes to the design were made throughout the period of construction. The thirteenth-century cathedral included nave, chancel, two pairs of transepts, a central crossing tower, an eastern chapel and retrochoir, and a north porch. The principal stone is a limestone quarried at Tisbury and Chilmark, some eleven miles away, which has weathered to grey-green on the exterior, but has remained cream inside. The predominant feature of the Early English design is the use of plain lancet windows, in twos and threes, repeated throughout the whole cathedral.

No-one is sure precisely when the upper stages of the tower and the spire were added, but the work was probably complete before 1330, so the entire cathedral may have been the achievement of no more than a century. Soaring spires were not an Early English feature, but the designer's skill in matching the architecture of the spire with that of the rest of the cathedral was such that a near-perfect unity was achieved. Two stages were added to the tower, which was then surmounted by a tapering octagonal spire, decorated up its angles with a profusion of ballflower ornament. Small spirelets fill the triangular spaces at the corners of the tower formed by the transition from square to octagon. The spire was by no means the tallest to have been built in England during the middle ages, but at 404 feet (123 metres) it is the tallest and, many would say, the most beautiful to have survived. An extensive programme of repair and restoration was carried out during the 1990s.

The addition of the spire imposed additional stresses on the existing structure, and flying buttresses projecting from the clerestory stage of the nave and chancel are external evidence of the remedial measures necessary to safeguard the building. These apart, the exterior

appearance of the cathedral has undergone very little change since the day in the fourteenth century when the capstone on top of the spire was put in place.

Now make your way into the cathedral, by whichever door is in use at the time of your visit. You will be asked to make a donation towards the cost of maintaining the fabric. Once inside stand at the west end of the nave.

It is not possible, within the confines of this book, to provide a comprehensive description of the architectural details and furnishings of Salisbury Cathedral. All that can be attempted are a few general observations, and brief mentions of some features which no visitor should miss. For more information a well-stocked bookshop will be found between the nave and the cloisters, and expert cathedral guides are on hand to answer questions.

Standing under the great triple-lancet west window it is possible to see the whole length of the cathedral, and the unity of its architecture is the most striking first impression. The uncluttered vista of Early English purity was enhanced (not without sacrifice) between 1788 and 1791 by the work of Bishop Barrington and James Wyatt, in removing or resiting many medieval and later accretions. The orderly arrangement of medieval tombs along the nave arcade plinths, for example, is the result of their tidying-up.

The second memorable impression is achieved by the use of two contrasting building stones. Creamy unweathered Chilmark or Tisbury is combined with another limestone, Purbeck marble, which in its natural state is dark grey, and polishes to almost black. Together the effect is of stunning beauty. The scheme of the design is very similar throughout. The arcade columns are of unpolished grey Purbeck decorated with vertical shafts of gleaming black. Above them the arches and spandrels are cream Chilmark. The next stage is a gallery or triforium, with two trefoil-headed openings beneath an arch in each bay, again in contrasting black and cream. Above the gallery is a clerestory stage with lancets. The vaults are not in fact very high, compared with some other cathedrals, but the effect of the polished Purbeck shafts in emphasizing the vertical is to create an impression of height.

If we now stroll around the cathedral interior in a clockwise direction, beginning at the western end of the north nave aisle, we soon arrive at the fourteenth-century clock from the demolished bell-tower, believed to be the oldest working clock in Europe. Nearby, on the arcade plinth, is a miniature bishop's tomb, probably made to cover the burial of just the deceased's heart. It was once thought to commemorate the death in office of a so-called 'boy-bishop', in fact a chorister who each Christmas was 'elected' bishop by his colleagues in an elaborate medieval custom of role-reversal.

As we move to the north transept we pass on the aisle wall monuments to victims of a railway disaster in 1906, and to Henry Hatcher, a celebrated local historian. More antiquaries, writers and historians are commemorated in the transept, including Sir Richard Colt Hoare, John Britton, Richard Jefferies and James 'Hermes' Harris. The crossing has a fifteenth-century vault and strainer arches, as well as a plumb mark on the floor, which was used to check for movement in the spire. The distortion caused by the additional weight of the tower and spire may be clearly seen by scrutinizing the crossing and transept columns.

We continue along the north choir aisle to the north-east transept, which contains a remarkably large brass to Bishop Wyville, who died in 1375, and a portion of the cathedral's medieval rood screen. Beyond, at the eastern end of the choir aisle is a mysterious seventeenth-century monument to Sir Thomas Gorges, builder of the equally mysterious Longford Castle. We have arrived at the ambulatory or retrochoir, supported by the slenderest of polished Purbeck columns, and, with the Trinity (or Lady) Chapel, the first portion of the cathedral to be completed. Overwhelming the visitor to the Trinity Chapel is its east window of modern glass, commemorating prisoners of conscience, which was completed in 1980. South of the retrochoir, corresponding with the Gorges monument, is another grandiose tomb, which commemorates the Earl of Hertford, Edward Seymour (he died in 1621), and members of his family.

From the south choir aisle we can gain access to the quire, which includes some early carved woodwork, although most is Victorian. The painted roundels decorating the vault are also Victorian, but they are approximate copies of the medieval originals. One represents Christ in glory, and others apostles and prophets, but the twelve to the east of Christ depict country scenes of the twelve months, such as digging, gathering fruit, and killing the pig.

Returning to the nave we find along the south arcade plinth more medieval tombs removed there by Wyatt. They may include Bishops Herman, Roger and Osmund, all brought from the cathedral at Old Sarum, and part of the shrine of St Osmund, with knee-holes where pilgrims could kneel in front of the saint's

effigy. The shrine originally stood in the Trinity Chapel at the cathedral's east end.

At the west end of the south aisle a doorway leads into the cloisters, which, as we have seen, are not an integral part of a secular cathedral such as Salisbury, but were included for liturgical or processional reasons. They also give access to the superb octagonal chapter house, with its central column of grey and black Purbeck, its generous windows, and its fascinating frieze of carvings depicting Old Testament scenes. The Salisbury copy of Magna Carta (one of only four survivors) is displayed in the chapter house. Two further bonuses for any visitor who ventures into the cloisters are the cedars of Lebanon which grace the cloister garth, as they have done since they were planted in 1837 to celebrate Victoria's accession.

Every cathedral, and indeed many a parish church, rewards its visitors in two ways. One is by the overwhelming impact of its architect's achievement, which at Salisbury, because of its unity, is perhaps more moving than in any other English cathedral. The other is by the accumulation of personal details, as revealed in the monuments and idiosyncrasies which adorn it, and which lurk in every corner for those who have the time and enthusiasm to search them out.

9 A WALK AROUND THE CITY

This walk explores some of the streets and buildings of Salisbury city centre, beginning and ending at the High Street Gate (see map page 72). It can be extended to take in also some of the eastern chequers.

Start by walking from High Street Gate along High Street to the first traffic lights, at the junction with New Street and Crane Street. Turn left into Crane Street.

The alignment of High Street probably coincides with an earlier route, in use before the city was established, which ran from Old Sarum to a river crossing at Aegel's Ford near Harnham Bridge. Buildings at this end of High Street include the S.P.C.K. premises (right, nearest the gate), a former inn which was used between the wars as the retail outlet for a local clothmaking initiative known as the 'Stonehenge Woollen Industry'. On the corner of High Street and New Street is Mitre House, another former inn – indeed most buildings in High Street have at some stage been inns, or occupy the sites of inns. A credible tradition asserts that this was the first plot to be built upon in the new city, and this is acknowledged by the practice of each new bishop robing here prior to his enthronement in the cathedral. Opposite, on the High Street–Crane Street corner (currently a restaurant), is an attractive fourteenth-century row of three timber-framed and jettied houses, with gables fronting High Street.

Walk along Crane Street until you reach the river at Crane Bridge.

Crane Street is named after a house (now Rechabite House), which was called the 'Crane' during the middle ages. Many houses in medieval cities, whether or not they were used as inns (in the modern sense), derived their name from some sign or badge displayed (like a logo) as a distinguishing mark. The road leads to the lower of the two bridges connecting the city with its older neighbour, the village of Fisherton Anger. On the left near the bridge is the suite of buildings now known as Church House, because since 1881 it has been used for diocesan administration. This is its third career. The

oldest part, the north range with the archway fronting the street, was built in the fifteenth century as the house of a wealthy clothier, William Lightfoot. He called it the 'Falcon', and later residential owners added the west range (facing the river). In 1638 it became the city workhouse, which was enlarged in 1728 by adding the south range (across the courtyard). Crane Bridge existed in the middle ages, but most of the present fabric is later, and the bridge has been widened twice during the last century. While here look back along Crane Street and its continuation, New Street. This may be the first artificial street line laid out when the city was being established, and it retains an almost straight alignment right across the city from west to east.

Cross Crane Street and walk along the riverside path, noting the information board about the river's wildlife. Halfway along cross the river by the modern footbridge and continue past the clock tower to stand on Fisherton Bridge.

The River Avon flows from various sources in the Vale of Pewsey, some twenty-five miles to the north of Salisbury. Not far below Crane Bridge it is augmented by the River Nadder (itself augmented by the Wylye), and lower still by the Bourne and the Ebble. These five rivers drain almost all of south and central Wiltshire. The Avon, thus enlarged, flows to the sea at Christchurch.

The river formed the boundary between medieval Salisbury and the parish of Fisherton Anger, but a suburb was encouraged to develop from an early date on the Fisherton side. Across the river between the two road bridges are the converted buildings of the former Salisbury Infirmary (closed in 1993), which have as their nucleus the original hospital of 1771. Next to Fisherton Bridge stands the clock tower of 1892, which is on the site of the medieval county gaol. The gaol was replaced in about 1840, but some masonry from it survives beneath the clock tower. Beyond Fisherton Bridge the main road out of the medieval city towards Wilton and Devizes is called Fisherton Street. Development along it had begun in the thirteenth century, with shops and a Dominican friary. Like High Street it later became lined with inns, and railway stations built at its far end in 1856-7 increased its importance. North of Fisherton Street large commercial malthouses were built during the nineteenth century, replacing and incorporating earlier maltings. During the 1970s and 1980s their site was redeveloped for shops, a car park, and theatre, the Salisbury Playhouse.

Fisherton Bridge was rebuilt in 1762 and 1872, and widened in 1960, so there is nothing medieval about it. An example of medieval superstition about rivers and river-crossings, however, came to light when the river and millstream were drained during 1987. More than two hundred metal pilgrim and secular badges and amulets were discovered in the stream-bed (some are now displayed in Salisbury Museum), presumably tossed into the water by their owners as thank-offerings for the safe return from the perils of numerous journeys and pilgrimages.

A little upstream from the bridge is the town or bishop's mill. The present eighteenth-century buildings, refurbished as a pub, occupy the site of a mill which probably existed at the time of Domesday Book, 1086 (some 150 years before the city was built). It was replaced with a new mill by Bishop Richard Poore, the city's founder, and during the sixteenth century and later there are references to its use for fulling cloth. From 1899 it was used to generate electricity.

From the bridge walk to the pedestrian crossing and cross the road. Turn right, so that you are walking back along Bridge Street towards the city centre. Opposite the end of High Street turn left into St Thomas's Square. After viewing St Thomas's Church from outside, enter by the west door.

The former County Hotel of 1874 (now Barclays Bank and the King's Head Inn), which occupies the south side of Bridge Street, is an indication of the city's growing tourist industry after the railways had arrived. St Thomas's Church was begun soon after the city was laid out, and originally stood at the western end of the open market place. But by the later middle ages its small churchyard had become fringed by houses and shops. Apart from the tower of about 1400, almost all the church dates from after 1448, when the previous chancel collapsed. It was fortunate that this event occurred when it did, because Salisbury was then at the peak of its prosperity as a centre of clothmaking and marketing. Consequently ample funds were available from wealthy merchants to pay for the magnificent Perpendicular building. The tower stands over a right of way, presumably in existence before the city, which continued northwards to Old Sarum and southwards along the line of High Street to the river-crossing. Running south a path and archway to the street survive, but the present nave of the church has blocked its way to the north.

The unwary visitor entering the church for the first time is in for a surprise. It is not the light, airy effect of the walls of glass created by the fifteenth-century architect, which could be anticipated from looking at the exterior. Rather it is the powerful statement of medieval belief,

the doom painting, which is depicted on the chancel wall, above and around the chancel arch. This painting, made in the late-fifteenth century, subsequently whitewashed and forgotten, rediscovered in 1819 and restored in 1881, repays a few minutes' undivided attention. Afterwards move to the chapel south of the chancel. This is William Swayne's chantry, and the guild chapel of the tailors, which was referred to in chapter five. Notice too the arcade between the chancel and this chapel, with an inscription recording John Nichol's gift to the church; and in the south aisle find Humphrey Beckham's fine joinery.

Leave the church and turn left, retracing your steps as far as the Bridge Street–High Street corner. Here turn left again and walk along Silver Street to the corner, where you will see the Poultry Cross on the opposite side of the road. Continue left around the corner into Minster Street and make your way to the open area known as the Cheesemarket on the left hand side at the far end.

As we approach the Poultry Cross we are walking into the commercial heart of the medieval market place. Symptomatic of a successful medieval town are the many tall houses on restricted sites which have developed from earlier rows of market stalls, and which have encroached on to the open market place. All the houses lining Silver Street and Minster Street are the result of this infilling process, and several have surviving architecture of the fifteenth century, when the city reached its zenith. One such house facing the Poultry Cross (3/5 Minster Street), which now comprises a jeweller's shop and the restaurant of the Haunch of Venison Inn, has a particularly well-documented history, enabling successive changes of use and ownership to be reconstructed from about 1600.

It was probably built for a merchant, since his mark is carved over an internal doorway, and has been reproduced above the jeweller's fascia. The Haunch of Venison Inn has an interesting, and intimate, unspoilt interior.

The hexagonal Poultry Cross is contemporary with the fifteenth-century houses, although there was an earlier high cross on the same site, and the present superstructure above roof level was added in 1852-4. The association with poultry results from overcrowding in the medieval market place, which led to the market for dairy products and some other foodstuffs being moved to the north end of Minster Street. That area henceforth became known as the Cheesemarket (though its cross has gone), and the Poultry Cross took its name from one of the commodities which remained on sale there.

The Cheesemarket is joined to St Thomas's Square by a path between buildings, and this is the northward continuation of the right of way which was extinguished by the rebuilding of the church nave. Flanking the path on the left (viewed from the Cheesemarket) is a house on the site of the citizen's first guildhall or council house, which rivalled the bishop's administration from his guildhall until a new council

house was completed in 1584. Flanking the path on the right is the front of a large building which was once an important inn, the Vine. But the most impressive structure facing the Cheesemarket now is the classical portico of the former market house. This was built in 1859 as an attempt (which proved successful) to enhance Salisbury's appeal as a marketing centre, at a time when railway travel was exposing the city to increased competition from its rivals. The rest of the market house was demolished in 1975 to make way for the public library.

From the Cheesemarket cross to the market place and walk diagonally to the guildhall beyond the line of trees in the opposite corner (on market days, Tuesday and Saturday, this may take some time).

The sight of Salisbury's ample market place, surrounded as it is by an assembly of buildings of many dates and styles, supervised by its noble guildhall, and watched over from a distance by the tower of St Thomas's and the cathedral spire, cannot fail to send a thrill of excitement through anyone interested in urban history. On market days the scene is more memorable still, and the sight of the Michaelmas fair, held here for a week each autumn, is unforgettable. It is hard, therefore, to visualize the even larger proportions of the market place as first laid out. The northern and eastern edges (Blue Boar Row and Queen Street) are original, but all the buildings along its southern and western edges are encroachments. On the west the market place probably extended beyond St Thomas's Church to the river, and on the south it continued to the line of New Canal (which we shall explore shortly). If all the encroachments were to be swept away – perish the thought – the market place would revert to being more than twice its present size.

The organization of the market place, and the various commodities bought and sold there, are described above, on pages 36-9. The present guildhall stands on the site of a building known as the bishop's guildhall. This was built during the first century of the city's existence, in order to supervise the market and administer the city on behalf of its owner, the bishop. It survived until 1787/8 when, along with small shops which had been built against its walls, it was demolished. Meanwhile, as the power of the citizens' body, which was known as the mayor and commonalty, gradually increased, so by 1584 they had built and occupied their own administrative building, the council house. This was positioned in front of the guildhall, approximately where the war memorial now stands. It was damaged by fire in 1780, and in consequence the bishop's permission was secured to demolish his guildhall, as well as the council house, and erect a new one. This was paid for by a local landowner and member of Parliament for the city, the second Earl of Radnor. It was built between 1787 and 1795, altered in 1825 and 1889, and refurbished in 1990/1. Since 1927 it has no longer been the home of local government, but its other role, as law courts, continues, and it also serves as the venue for many local functions.

Although our walk now takes us back towards the High Street, visitors may wish to investigate the market place area further before resuming this walk. Three buildings may be of particular interest. William Russel's House (Watsons, 9 Queen Street) is a well-preserved house of 1306-14, with much original woodwork visible inside the shop. The modern Cross Keys development of shops (opening off Queen Street) incorporates a seventeenth-century staircase to the gallery of the former Plume of Feathers Inn, whose yard has been partially recreated in the modern architecture. The surviving range of the Boar Inn, which was built in 1444, and for which the written building contract survives, is now the restaurant within Debenham's department store.

If time permits, a more adventurous excursion could be made at this point in the walk. Queen Street is part of an almost straight alignment extending from north to south right through the medieval city. Running north from the market place it is called Endless Street, and to the south it includes Catherine Street and Exeter Street (which we encountered on our walk around the Close). In the area to the east of this road line (that is, behind Queen Street and its continuations) lie most of the so-called 'chequers', roughly rectangular blocks formed by a grid of streets. These should be explored at leisure, and if possible the visitor should venture to both the northern and southern limits of this area. To the north is the former St Edmund's Church, which is now an arts centre, and next to it is the Council House, or Bourne Hill. This is essentially a sixteenth-century residence built on the site of the collegiate buildings attached to the church; since 1927 it has been the offices of the city (and now district) council, and its south front looks out over an area known as the Greencroft, the principal communal open space within the area of the medieval city. At the southern end of the eastern chequers runs St Ann Street, which possesses good houses of many periods and styles, including the elaborately carved joiners' hall. Until the ring road was constructed it used to carry Southampton-bound traffic out of the city, but now it is a quiet backwater, with an elegant view down its length to the cathedral. After these optional deviations the visitor should return to the Guildhall and resume the walk.

Go round to the rear of the Guildhall (Fish Row), and make your way along Butcher Row towards the Poultry Cross. Just before reaching the cross turn left beside a spectacular timber-framed goldsmith's shop, and you will find yourself in an open area bordering the street known as New Canal.

Fish Row and Butcher Row are good examples of market infill, their names signifying the tradesmen located there. Ox Row and Oatmeal Row have also survived, but many others which are recorded in documents have been forgotten, including rows in the Poultry Cross area for pots

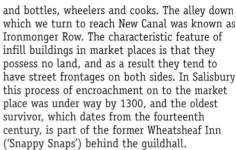

and bottles, wheelers and cooks. The alley down which we turn to reach New Canal was known as Ironmonger Row. The characteristic feature of infill buildings in market places is that they possess no land, and as a result they tend to have street frontages on both sides. In Salisbury this process of encroachment on to the market place was under way by 1300, and the oldest survivor, which dates from the fourteenth century, is part of the former Wheatsheaf Inn ('Snappy Snaps') behind the guildhall.

The name of New Canal reminds us that from its foundation until the nineteenth century Salisbury had open watercourses running along many of its streets. The largest of these was known as the town ditch, and this was also the common name given to the original southern edge of the market place, along which it flowed, and which is now marked by New Canal. The town ditch was the last watercourse to be filled in; it went in 1875.

This area was popular with merchants and gentry, probably because of the generous proportions of the gardens behind the houses along the southern side of the street. Many houses which retained medieval features were demolished during the 1960s, but the most celebrated, the Hall of John Halle, has survived, although its present use as a cinema foyer is bizarre. It was built as the showpiece house of one of Salisbury's most powerful fifteenth-century merchants, but its present appearance owes much to restorations in 1834 and 1880, as well as to its current use. The internal decoration of the art deco cinema behind it takes its cue from John Halle's medieval architecture, and its preservation has been vigorously defended.

Behind Butcher Row there is an open area adjacent to New Canal. This has been the wood and coal market, and also a pig market; it is now used by taxis and village buses. To its west, extending as far as High Street, is another block of market infill known as Mitre Chequer. It includes a nineteenth-century tea warehouse which retains its hoist.

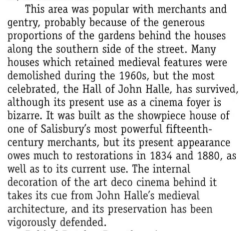

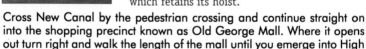

Cross New Canal by the pedestrian crossing and continue straight on into the shopping precinct known as Old George Mall. Where it opens out turn right and walk the length of the mall until you emerge into High Street.

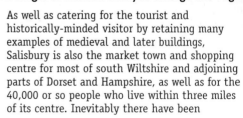

As well as catering for the tourist and historically-minded visitor by retaining many examples of medieval and later buildings, Salisbury is also the market town and shopping centre for most of south Wiltshire and adjoining parts of Dorset and Hampshire, as well as for the 40,000 or so people who live within three miles of its centre. Inevitably there have been pressures to redevelop the city centre, and Old George Mall is an example dating from 1967.

It takes its name from the George Inn, probably the most important of the medieval inns fronting High Street. Its history is extremely well documented from 1361 onwards, principally because it passed into the ownership of the mayor and commonalty during the fifteenth century, and remained in their hands until 1858. The façade and parts of the upper floors fronting the street have been retained, along with some of their internal woodwork; but the yard, and the various interesting buildings surrounding it, were all replaced by the 1960s shopping precinct.

Turn left, and walk back along High Street to the gate.

This completes our stroll around Salisbury city centre, but it has had to omit many buildings and places of interest, especially those on the fringes. Harnham Mill, which is approached via Crane Bridge Road, Elizabeth Gardens and the Town Path, makes a pleasant walk and an interesting destination, with fine views of the cathedral across the meadows. St Martin's Church, now severed from the city by the ring road, is too seldom visited. The site of medieval Clarendon Palace, recently cleared and excavated, is accessible by heading eastwards from the city and across Milford Bridge. The village of Bemerton, on the western outskirts, boasts the church and rectory where the poet George Herbert ministered in the seventeenth century. And of course a pilgrimage to the hillfort, castle and cathedral at Old Sarum is essential, for that is where the whole story began.

INDEX